Introduction to Backpacking

Introduction to Backpacking

By

Robert Colwell

Illustrated by
Harold Nosti

STACKPOLE BOOKS

INTRODUCTION TO BACKPACKING

Copyright © 1970 by
Robert Colwell

Published by
STACKPOLE BOOKS
Cameron and Kelker Streets
Harrisburg, Pa. 17105

Printed in U.S.A.

To
Jo Ann,
who walked the miles with me

Contents

Introduction

BACKPACKING can be a summer-long adventure or a memorable weekend outing, a month spent hiking a famous trail or a few pleasant days in a nearby forest. Either way it will be an exhilarating outdoor encounter. With this in mind the following pages were written, introducing those newly interested to backpacking, while providing expert reference for those already involved. The emphasis will be on the short trip, in the belief that this is most popular with beginners and experienced alike.

No one can have a successful backpacking trip without proper preparation. A weekend hike is not a small undertaking, and a four-day family outing requires considerable planning. Thorough efforts before starting will make the difference between a carefree holiday and a miserable experience.

Here is a step-by-step advisor for those with limited background or a helpful guide for those seeking tips and hints on ways to get more out of their backpacking trips. Follow this book through preparation, outfitting, a day on the trail, campfire cooking, wilderness nights, and subsequent planning of longer trips.

Tips on unique backpacking situations will help avoid wrong trip choices, bad hiking habits, or the tendency to overload. Tables and diagrams will assist in choosing the right equipment, proper menus, and campsites. Why backpacking, how to hike, where to hike—they are all in the following pages.

chapter one

The Sport of Backpacking

HENRY David Thoreau believed that in the woods one would encounter the essential facts of life. There he could learn what the wilderness had to teach and would not, when he came to die, discover that he had not lived. There are other reasons as compelling: health, recreation, stimulation, and appreciation—all ingredients of a life style that insists we engage the wilderness and savor its meaning to us.

Certainly those who backpack are seeking an experience out of the ordinary, be they conservationists, hunters, businessmen or ecologists, housewives or retirees. All have in common a desire to broaden their experience horizon. Every one of them feels the need to keep in touch with his natural environment. But only a few spend the greater part of their lives outdoors, while most struggle to secure an occasional few days or weeks away from office and home. Nevertheless, their excursions into the wilderness are needed times of revitalization of spirit and body—a reaffirmation of self-reliance and confidence.

Unlike the cliché that describes those who scale heights because the peaks are there, other men pack into the wilderness not so much because *it* is there but because *they* want to be there. It is the doing of it that counts. And that exciting involvement is the stimulus that leads a group of Girl Scouts to be on the trail for five consecutive weekends, or draws other men 3,000 miles to join a four-day hike in the Sierras.

The ranks of backpackers teem with such individuals. More often than not they have evolved from a camper or a sportsman. With a taste for the outdoors already familiar to them, these outdoor people, now backpackers, are developing their experience still further. They have recognized the limits of their previous involvement; campgrounds are becoming overcrowded parks, while game preserves are being overshot and lakes overfished. Seeking that solitary respite that can no longer be found otherwise, they are taking to wilderness trails for pleasure and game.

And their welcome is loud to anyone who will join them. With or without a camping background, no one should hesitate to take that first trip into the wilderness. Nothing about backpacking makes such a goal the least bit difficult to accomplish. A day on the trail will breed the necessary confidence. To get started check with friends; there is bound to be an outdoor man amongst them. Conversation with a hiker or camper will produce enough information for initial planning. Write for catalogs, talk to the salesman at a local sport store. Make the commitment to backpack and follow through.

Family Fun

There is no finer way to enjoy backpacking than on a family basis. What better way to introduce children to their natural environment? Or for parents to enjoy a child's wonderment at new surroundings? What better way to experience the pleasure of such close comradery? Backpacking is unique in this sense. Alone in the wilderness a family finds new meaning to their existence as a unit. A recess from the usual press of timetables and responsibility is satisfying beyond measure. More tangible benefits are also to be had by family backpackers. The community use of kitchen gear, food, and tents will allow for lessening of individual loads. And parents need not consider toddlers a handicap. A thirty-pound child is easily carried on specially designed packframes (see Chapter 3).

Alone or in a Group

A family can go it alone into the forest or, as individuals and couples, they can consider going with others. Group backpacking will mean especially good times. There is no better way for those thinking of their first backpacking trip. Organized trail hikes are sponsored by many groups like the Sierra Club and the Florida Trail Association (see Chapter 12 for addresses). Boy Scouts and other youth groups provide an excellent approach for anyone interested in working with youngsters.

While group hiking usually imposes restrictions of time, duration, and route, this is offset by the enjoyment of meeting new and stimulating personalities. There is security in numbers, usually reinforced by the presence of others with experience and knowledge. Moreover, like family backpacking, group packing allows loads to be lessened if the concepts of community kitchen and food stores are employed.

Physical Shape and Attitudes

The physical requirements for backpacking are minimal. No special physical attributes make this one a backpacker and that one not. Any healthy body can withstand the rigors of a weekend outdoors in the forest—and should seek it! Long legs, a strong back, and good feet are sure to be helpful, but the latter two can be developed by anyone.

Perhaps of paramount importance are mental attitudes. Start a trip without misgivings; be confident that planning and preparation are adequate. Take heart in the knowledge that once on the trail dreams are being realized. This is the doing of it, the very involvement with life and environment that sets a man on the trail apart from others, and makes him much richer for the experience.

Age Is No Handicap

If the physical requirements can be met, there is no need to hesitate because of age. Youngsters or oldsters alike can take to the trail with confidence, perhaps limiting their objectives while savoring fully their outdoor encounter. Senior citizens with walking histories will readily adapt to backpacking, while the small fry often have enough energy to outlast anyone. While observing limits of endurance is prudent here, age should not be a barrier.

Go Light and Comfortable

Make an early decision to go light and comfortable. Fifty pounds on the back does not make for easy going; yet many hikers start off with a burden like this. It is soon unbearable. Their struggle becomes a misery that affects others in the party. Nothing else will ruin a trip quicker.

Overloading demonstrates bad judgment. It is unnecessary, considering the availability of lightweight equipment.

Some backpackers keep their basic gear load under twenty pounds and can spend a summer week in the wilderness (warm, dry, and full) with less than twenty-five pounds on their back. The idea here is to be adequately equipped with self-sufficient, yet light gear. There are no medals for great loads carried, only aching muscles and fatigue.

Minimize Equipment Needs

To maintain this "go light and comfortable" policy, back-packers are constantly thinking of ways to reduce loads. And the easiest way to accomplish this is to minimize equipment needs. Look over a gear list carefully. Evaluate. *Need* is the main criteria, and need means utility and comfort. Now cut. Be firm and discard with confidence. Ounces saved in clothing or cooking gear will be important.

Gear lists for short trips can be especially spare. Family and group backpacking will allow for load sharing of community items. However, do not become obsessed with the idea of gear paring. Too much time can be spent calculating ounces to be saved or regretting decisions that let you include an extra item. Once an acceptable load is decided on, then consider if the price of adding any item is worth it. Usually it is not, especially after once taking to the trail with a light pack.

Lighter with the Right Gear

Another way to go light is to purchase specialized ultra-lightweight equipment. A good deal of backpacking gear can be found at local sport stores or obtained from either of the two giant mail order houses in America. Unfortunately, these outlets are frequently understocked or provide only the less expensive and heavier gear designed more for hunters and campers. The nature of backpacking requires special equipment to be purchased mostly from companies that manufacture this gear (see Chapter 12 for list of suppliers). It does make the difference. However, while this approach lightens the load it also lightens the pocketbook. But consider the investment worth it. This is superior equipment, designed for long wear and the convenience of light weight.

chapter two

A Backpacking Trip

PLANNING and preparation are the necessary foundations of any successful backpacking trip. And these first steps can be an exciting time when ideas and imagination merge to heighten anticipation for that moment when the trip starts. However, it is a time when decisions are made that will make the difference between a good trip or a bad one; so give every consideration to all phases of planning and preparation.

All Seasons for Backpackers

Choosing a time to backpack is simply a matter of preference. Any season can be enjoyed so long as the proper equipment is used. By far most backpacking is done during the summer months in the western mountains. However, do not overlook the fall trip when leaves are changing in the Appalachians, or the inviting sunny days to be spent on the Florida Trail in midwinter. And snow trips are something to contemplate as experience matures.

When choosing a time keep in mind that in the east and north June is the month for nagging insects, while in some western states snow still covers the trails. And midsummer heat in Florida makes hikers turn to canoe trips on wild rivers. Check a guidebook for weather to be expected in areas of interest. This will allow for plans that will more reasonably anticipate good weather periods.

Careful consideration should be taken when choosing a route during fall and winter. Many areas are crowded with hunters then.

Guides and Maps

Maps and guidebooks must be sent for. Select an area of interest: mountains, prairies, hills, or savannahs. Narrow it down to a state, or better yet a national forest or wilderness area, and write to the appropriate agency for detailed maps. So much the better if the choice is in an area covered by maps and guides supplied by organizations like the Appalachian Trail Conference or the Florida Trail Association. These are very complete. Local sport stores, equipment suppliers' catalogs, and the library are sure to have lists of fine guidebooks and maps, some with cursory information and others with great detail.

While obtaining this advance information is the best method of preparation, it is not always feasible. For instance, when vacationing by car and suddenly making the decision to hike in an unfamiliar area, you will probably not have the background information. Get in touch with the nearest

National Forest District ranger. The rangers have good maps, usually free. National parks also have maps and guidebooks for sale at their visitor centers. Often the man behind the desk will have covered the trails in the area of interest. This kind of information can be invaluable.

Getting in Shape

While waiting for those guidebooks and maps, start a program of physical conditioning that will allow for a few days' backpacking without the misery of aching muscles. To accomplish this there is little else to do but walk. Start with short walks, but be determined. No strolling around the block. Decide on how many miles and make it regular; an evening walk, perhaps. Over hills if possible, with vigor for sure!

Apartment dwellers and those who work in office buildings may want to forgo the convenience of elevators. Walking up and down stairs is excellent practice for those planning mountain hiking. Bicycling is also good preparation. If practical, wear hiking boots, those that will be used on the trail. The important thing is to strengthen legs and toughen feet. Perhaps conditioning can be accomplished along with those who are to be trail companions.

Alone or with Companions

While hiking alone can be extremely rewarding, backpacking with others is the safest way to hike. In family and group packing the choice of companions is already made, but selecting a good companion is not difficult. Anyone who enjoys this mutual experience is usually congenial and helpful.

These outings become team efforts in a loose sense, so there is a need for a semblance of authority and responsibility in the party. Companions may consider and debate, but decisions should have the approval of a leader. Experience is the main criterion for leadership, and someone in the party should be recognized as being in charge. In a situation where all are without much background let the responsibility fall to the man considered to have the best judgment.

Selecting Routes and Destinations

Once guidebooks and maps are in hand, attention can be focused on selecting a route. Determine a base camp. Can the trail be reached from there by hiking? Must a car be used? Next note the terrain. In mountains calculate the net feet of ascent and descent and, if possible, hike *downhill*. Consider a trail with the fewest ascents and descents. Try to hike the steep section of a trail during the first half of any trip. Keep the hot afternoon sun at your back; hike from south to north, or west to east. Become familiar with possible campsites and water sources. Be flexible; think of alternate routes or spurs that may become just as inviting as the first route choice.

Hard Hike or Stroll

A very important decision now is the type of hike to plan. How many miles a day? Will it be a hard hike or a stroll? Both have their place. Experience favors something in between, especially where families and groups are concerned. Physical conditioning can also limit the pace and, to a large extent, trail terrain dictates the mileage. Only four or five miles a day when steep climbing is not unusual, or fifteen miles a day downhill or over prairies is quite an acceptable goal. However, anyone wanting to thoroughly enjoy the environment will try to keep daily mileage at six to eight miles. This usually provides time enough for photography, vista gazing, and perhaps a nap at lunch or a few fly casts into a lake. This is what backpacking is all about.

Day Trip

While selecting routes a decision as to trip duration must be made. First to be considered might be the day trip. Choose a route with a lake at the site of a lunch stop. Others might consider a mountaintop a good halfway point. As a trial plan, take along a loaded pack. Share the carrying of it. Get accustomed to the burden and see if gear paring has been adequate. If the decision is to go light, most of what will be needed will fit in a knapsack. Take along a camera or fishing rod and plan to relax for an hour or two at lunch. When traveling light, with an early start, ten miles should be the limit.

If time permits on a vacation, a day trip is an excellent way to become acclimatized to higher altitudes. These trips in themselves are immensely rewarding. They will also put the final touches to a program of physical conditioning.

Overnight Trip

After one or two day trips it will be time to plan the first overnight outing. It can be return trip, but one-way hikes are more interesting. This usually requires ferrying a car for pickup service, unless the route is a loop hike. However, more often than not an hour of driving in the morning, or evening before, will have a car many more miles away than can be hiked in two days. Another solution is to plan to end a hike at a campground or public area where transportation can be easily bought.

Make this first hike at a leisurely pace. Pick a route that will not be arduous; six to eight miles a day are plenty, especially on mountain trails or through brush. On overnight trips gambling on the weather is a reasonable way to lighten loads.

Long Weekend Trips

With the overnight trip now history, the long weekend trip becomes feasible. A three-day hike of 20-25 miles can take a backpacker into very remote areas. The experience of past day trips and overnight outings will come into full use. Careful planning of menus is important. Be prepared for weather changes, and still try to choose a route within everyone's capabilities.

As an alternate consider one day for hiking in, a day's layover at a particularly pleasant spot—lake, mountain slope, or meadow—in order to fish or explore, then a return on the third day. With this as a plan the daily mileage might be stretched to ten miles. Here again a one-way trip should be planned if possible.

Backpacking Near Home

All too often it seems that backpacking trips take us to areas of our nation many miles from home. However, not to be overlooked are the possibilities of trips in our own backyard. Many state and national forests, though small in area, provide trails readily followed. These are excellent proving grounds for beginners. Often these forests are secluded enough to provide good backpacking country. Moreover, these trails can be just what is needed for a pleasant day hike or conditioning hike for those longer trips contemplated.

Something More Than Hiking

Try not to allow backpacking to become an end in itself. It should only be a means to an end. Wilderness contact is the primary concern. Study the recreation possibilities on the trail. Fishing, photography, or bird-watching can provide hours of enjoyment. Studying flora and fauna can prove immensely interesting. Become familiar with the history and geology of the area hiked. Discussions of these topics are most rewarding, and you will be pleasantly surprised to learn how much there still is to learn.

Now with the planning and preparation well underway, it is time to seriously consider equipment needs.

chapter three

Packing It All
On Your Back

HOW best to carry the gear needed for any trip is of vital interest to the backpacker. The choice of packs should be made only after careful consideration of needs. Of primary concern is how much will be carried. Every effort should be made to keep pack loads at a reasonable weight—a different amount for everyone. Certainly a big man can handle heavy loads; yet there is no reason he should. Thirty pounds should be the limit for most men on a typical summer backpacking trip.

It is a good idea to establish acceptable load limits for women and children. Fill up a pack and have them carry it on a day hike. As a guide use a limit of 20 pounds for women and 15 pounds for children. Comfort is the aim, and with a well-thought-out gear list it will not be too difficult to reduce loads.

Backpacks have evolved from the likes of over-the-shoulder sacks, duluth-type packs complete with tumplines, heavy rucksacks, and frame packs to the now universal packframe and bag that allows a backpacker to carry great loads with none of the discomfort and fatigue caused by the other packs. However, these packframes were designed before the advent of popular, low-cost, lightweight gear. Moreover, and more dramatically, the development of freeze-dried food has greatly lessened the space requirement in packs. It is now possible to adequately feed a person with less than 1 1/2 pounds of food per day. It remains expensive, yet well worth the cost, considering the appreciable weight savings.

It now seems there is no longer reason to accept the packframe and bag (4 lbs.) as standard gear for packing loads if the weight is reduced to the point where two people can pack into the wilderness for a three-day summer hike with only 27 pounds of gear and food (see Chapter 9). Serious consideration should be given to substituting a day pack or small rucksack as the basic carrying gear in a backpacker's equipment. They are half the weight and much easier to handle when loaded with not more than 15-20 pounds.

However, remember that volume, not weight, can be the deciding factor in a choice of packs. For instance, cold-weather backpacking that requires bulky down clothing, stoves, tents, etc., will certainly require packframes and bags. For this reason a basic decision must be made as to what kind of trips will be contemplated. Summer hikes in the mountains, desert, or prairies? Winter hikes in Florida? Fall or spring trips that require a certain amount of cold-weather gear? For very active backpackers, perhaps it will be necessary to have more than one type of bag.

Packs and Frames

As with much of the gear available today—clothing, sleeping bags, shelters—there are many types and sizes to choose from, each designed to do specific service under certain conditions.

Frameless Packs

These small packs are shoulder suspended and fit snug against the back. Usually they provide up to 1500 cubic inches with a recommended 20-pound top loading. They are ideal for use when only packing a lunch and sweater, etc. A teardrop-shaped bag is excellent for rock climbing where maneuverability is at a premium. All of these small bags fold and store easily in a larger pack, making them excellent bags for day hikes away from a base camp. They are quite adequate packs for small children learning to do their part on a family outing. Two of these packs are all that is needed for a couple on a long weekend hike, provided they have designed their gear list around lightweight equipment and food.

Good day packs will feature leather bottoms, waterproof nylon material, felt-padded leather straps, D-ring suspension for hoisting the bag about, waist straps, and rustproof fittings. They weigh about 1 1/2 pounds. The disadvantage of these packs is their snug fit to the back; they can be hot. And care must be taken to properly store hard items to the outside of the pack.

Frame Packs

These larger packs or rucksacks are usually fitted with some type of frame between the pack and back. The frame

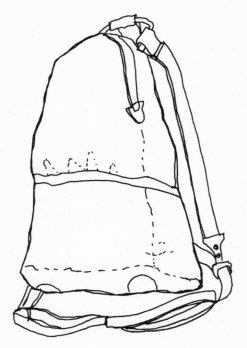

Frameless Pack

can be molded plastic, wood, or metal. They are shoulder-suspended, narrow, and fit close to the body. The frame provides a certain amount of ventilation and keeps hard items off the back. A recommended load range of 15-30 pounds is plenty, while the volume provided will be between 1000-2000 cubic inches. Consider these packs for moderate loads in skiing, climbing, trail working, or use in high winds.

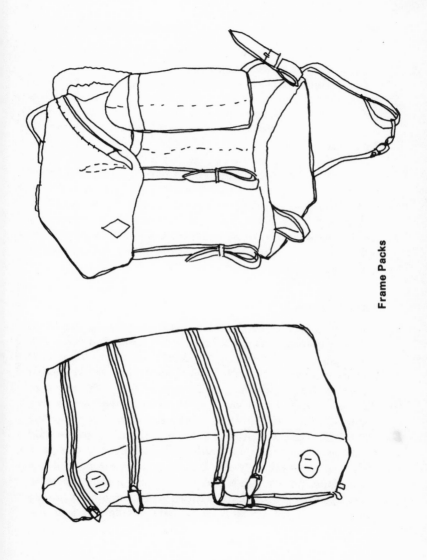

Frame Packs

One of these combined with a day pack will be adequate for a couple on a week-long trip.

Good frame packs will have the same design features as day packs described above. In addition, some packs have outer pockets for convenience, while others feature ski-carrying slots behind those pockets. They weigh about 2 pounds.

However, some rucksacks can be quite heavy. Cotton-duck, leather straps, fittings, and frame can weigh as much as 4 pounds, the weight of a complete packframe and bag. Moreover, they are not too comfortable when loads get above 30 pounds. The center of gravity is then far enough back of the wearer to cause uncomfortable strain to shoulders and back. This hastens fatigue. At this point, it is advisable to consider a packframe.

Packframes

Whereas the rucksack is European in origins, the light-weight packframe and packbag is an American idea and development. For carrying moderate to heavy loads (30 pounds and up) it is the only equipment to consider. A welded aluminum frame designed as a flattened S fits the curve of the back, while nylon webbing bands stretched across the frame keep it off the back. Padded straps pull it to the shoulders, while a waist band cinched tight brings the load to the hips. Rather than loading the shoulders, the pack weight is transferred to the legs, the strongest part of the body. Padded waist bands make the cinching more comfortable. The load is essentially vertical, and the center of gravity close to the packer's back and easily handled. Adopt this

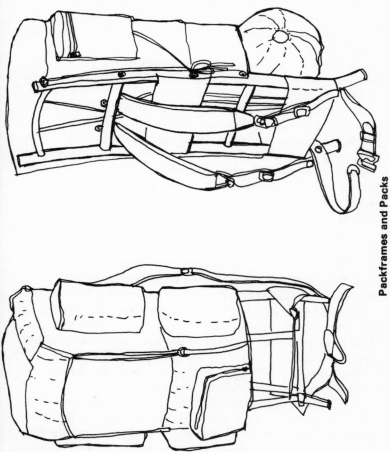

Packframes and Packs

method, if possible, over the practice of hanging the load from the shoulders and using the waist band only as a securer. It may seem a little uncomfortable at first, but in the long run it reduces fatigue.

Packbags to fit these lightweight frames hold from 1500 to 3700 cubic inches and can take very heavy loads—60 pounds or more. Generally, the bigger the bag, the better. The weight difference between a medium- and large-size bag can be as little as 2 ounces. A wide variety of bags are available, most of them of good design and construction. The best bags feature waterproof nylon duck that will take the beating of brush and rocks, covered zippers, as many as 6 pockets for convenience, and 2 or more separate main compartments. Equipment can easily be lashed to the outside. Nearly all are designed to fit high on frames, allowing sleeping bags to be lashed to the bottom behind the waist.

Make sure the bag fastens securely to your frame. Some bags have top pockets that fit snugly over the extended upper legs of a packframe. They also tie at the bottom of the frame. Another popular arrangement is a series of grommets or clevis pins that fasten the bag to the length of the packframe's outer legs. Both are reliable.

A large complete packframe and bag seldom weighs less than 4 pounds.

Because of their larger size, packframes will sometimes present a hazard while hiking. They can catch on brush and prevent ducking under fallen trees, or knock the wearer off balance when the pack above shoulder height bumps into trees or rocks. Once off balance, a struggling backpacker can sustain muscle strains trying to right himself. In high winds they offer more area to the wind force.

Remember it is essential to use the waistbelt. Keep it tight, even though at first it may feel uncomfortable. Hoist the pack higher on the back and cinch in; let the load come to hips and legs.

The Packframe When It Is Not a Packframe

Any packframe and bag can act as a weather wall in an open fly shelter. The frames also make good stretcher-type carriers for bringing wood from other areas. Possibly their best use is as a comfortable backrest once laid up against a rock or tree. Use them this way for all rest stops. Disengage from the pack and relax completely.

Hoisting a Pack

The simplest way to get a pack on is to have someone else hold it and then slip into the straps. If alone or just plain independent, try using a fallen tree or rock ledge to position the pack higher. That failing, sit down, hook up, and get up from a hands-and-knees position.

If the pack is light enough, just swing it up to a raised thigh, placing one strap on the shoulder as your arm goes through. Holding the bottom leg of the frame, hoist a bit higher and slip the other arm through the strap.

Other Packs

Handy beltpacks are excellent for personal items, photo equipment, and the like. Made of waterproof nylon with covered zipper openings, they either clip to a belt or have their own belt.

Every supplier can furnish a variety of sizes in waterproof stuff sacks with drawstring closures. One company has designed bags to straddle a dog's back.

A guide and map pocket that fits on packframe straps at the chest is a worthy attachment for keeping track of pens, thermometers, paper, maps, etc.

Backpacking with a Baby

Manufacturers have made it possible for a baby to go along on all family outings. Papoose-style frames allow the child to sit in comfort while reducing fatigue for the carrier. Front-facing chairs tend to be hot with baby leaning against the carrier. Rear-facing chairs move the center of gravity further away from the carrier's back because of the baby's tendency to lean forward. Some models of these seats can be obtained to adapt to regular packframes.

Filling the Pack

Some people pay little attention to packing. Others start with good intentions, become frustrated and impatient with the need to be systematic, and just chuck the whole idea and stuff things into the bag as do the first group. Still others pack and unpack carefully, observing the rules of proper packing. Theory has it that heavy items should be packed highest; however, with modern gear it becomes difficult to find heavy items. A stove weighs the same as a poncho, as do a small camera and a down jacket. Consider packing small, heavy items on top and large, bulky items lower. Keep the hard objects off the inside back when using a rucksack. Get as many things of constant use into the outside pockets. Practice will soon determine the best approach. At any rate, develop a system and use it always. This will come in handy in the dark. It will save the need to open 6 pockets and a main compartment to find the toilet paper.

chapter four

Trail
Footwear

WHAT to put on your feet for the trail is debated whenever hikers gather. It has never been resolved to satisfy everyone, nor is that likely to ever happen. We do know that feet take the load of body and gear for many hours at a stretch while backpacking. They perspire freely, get wet easily, and are difficult to keep warm. Certainly it is in our best interest to treat them as best we can. What follows is a reasonable evaluation of different footwear. There will be no attempt to discuss hiking in street shoes and sandals, or those people who hike barefoot.

Sneakers

The ubiquitous sneaker is the choice of many. They are light but not durable, get wet easily yet dry quickly. Considering the cost and weight saving over leather boots, you can afford several pairs—a factor for a family to consider. However,

they offer little support for feet while carrying a heavy pack.
They can be uncomfortable on rocky trails and they offer no
protection from outboard ankle scrapes and bruises. Ground
briers will tear them apart. If they are to be used, get the
high-top models.

Work Boots

Commonplace lightweight work boots or outdoor boots are
preferred by many, especially for children or where the trail
is easy going. They can be kept waterproof, and the uppers
are quite durable. They are comfortable and require very
little breaking in. However, the crepe soles wear fast,
although they can be resoled at a reasonable price. They
cost about a third the price of good hiking boots. A variety
featuring kangaroo leather uppers cost as much as hiking
boots; yet the soles are not at all comparable.

Thermal Boots

For backpackers planning to hike very wet trails in spring, or
those headed through swampy lake country, the traditional
high-top hunting boots with rubber bottoms and leather
uppers might be considered. Wear them with felt insoles and
heavy socks. Arch supports may be necessary for those who
cannot accept the flat foot feeling of rubber boots.

New models of this boot type feature insulated vibram
soles for hiking in icy water. These are the thermal boots
made with a sandwich layer on rubber and closed cell foam.
However, they are not recommended for hiking great dis-
tances.

Another way to achieve the same insulation in rubber boots is to use plastic bags as a vapor barrier: bare feet, plastic bag, 2 pairs wool socks, plastic bag, felt or mesh insoles, and then boots. Feet will be very moist; however, there will be very little heat loss due to damp socks carrying off the perspiration.

Hiking Boots

Expertly designed and made hiking boots provide incomparable trail footwear. These boots insulate well on either the frozen ground or a hot, sandy trail. They offer positive protection for your foot when stepping on rocks and roots, something that can be painful and bruising with any other type of footwear, and they provide secure footing on wet stones, moss, mud, and snow, thus lessening the chance of a sprain or ankle twist. However, until they are broken in they usually feel heavy and cumbersome. There is also the risk of blisters at this time.

First decide what service is wanted from hiking boots. Will it be casual day hikes, long pack trips, wet-weather trekking, or rock climbing? No one boot satisfies all conditions, but there is sure to be one boot that will give optimum service under the conditions generally hiked.

Look for boots with few seams in the uppers. They will be easier to keep waterproof and mean construction with fewer weak points. Get boots with complete leather lining and padded tongues and ankles. A steel shank and thick vibram lug soles are essential for good wear on rough hiking. Seldom are these boots more than 7 inches high. Nor should any hiking boot be higher than 8 inches. Anything more begins to restrict calf muscles.

Be sure to select the right weight boot. Light construction may mean weak boots, while too heavy a boot will mean unnecessary weight. Uppers should be strong enough to support the foot muscles straining under the extra weight of a pack; yet they must give slightly to the pressures of walking.

Selecting boots can be a difficult task, especially when ordering by mail. However many boots are sold this way and most suppliers do their best to satisfy. Catalogs describe models and styles very well, honestly listing advantages and features while not attempting to hide limits. Rely on them to provide a good fit.

Sizing and Fitting

In sizing boots remember that feet swell once on the trail and under a pack load. Allow for this. Make a foot silhouette drawing and send it along with the order. Use regular shoe size and measurements only for a point of departure. And do not be reluctant to return boots that do not fit. Select boots by how comfortable they feel, not the size; boot sizes can vary widely.

When standing and wearing customary hiking socks, laced-up boots should fit snugly, while leaving a finger's width between toes and the boot toe (stick a finger between heel and boot). Toes should be able to wiggle freely, and the ball of the foot should not feel pinched. The heel should barely be able to move; walking about should not allow the heel to move up and down nor the foot to slide forward to pinch toes.

Good boots will be stiff, a consideration in evaluating a fit as well as when breaking them in. And they will remain uncomfortable for awhile. Wax them well; then start regular short walks—the best way to become accustomed to new boots. Wearing them around the house will hasten this procedure. Practice hikes with full pack will toughen feet and legs. Most hiking trips are associated with a day or so of trail-head camping. Wear new boots then.

Insoles

Boots can be more comfortable with insoles that insulate, take the edge off rough stitching (unlined boots), and reduce foot fatigue. Felt, foam, and nylon mesh are used. Soft leather over foam is very satisfactory. Nylon mesh are the coolest and dryest. Felt can become saturated with foot moisture that may lead to cold feet. Most insoles can be trimmed to fit boots. Do not glue them in so that they cannot easily be replaced.

Laces

Very strong round or flat nylon laces are preferred. The weather does not take its toll of them as it does with leather laces.

Boot Care

The proper care of leather boots is essential. Regular attention will keep leather uppers waterproof and supple. However, a completely waterproof boot is not the goal; that would make for very hot feet. Sealed joints and seams are what a hiker wants. When boots look dirty, clean them with saddle soap; then coat with any of the waterproofing compounds available. Be sure to use patience; rub deep into seams and the uppers-sole joint. Do not use animal fat or grease. On the trail, in rain or excessive dew, boots may need coating every few days.

Dry wet boots slowly. Stuff them with newspaper or clothes and keep them away from a fire. Quick drying can ruin boots. Keep in mind, too, that wearing them until they are dry is not all that uncomfortable in mild weather.

Before storing boots, clean them a final time with saddle soap, oil them, and pack with newspaper or use boot stretchers. Find a high, dry place for them, where rodents cannot get at the laces if they are leather.

When it is time, have boots resoled by an expert. Some backpacking suppliers offer this service, or Vibram soles can be purchased through catalogs and the work done by a local shoe repair store.

Camp Shoes

Shedding trail boots and stepping into comfortable camp shoes can be a delightful experience. Tired sore feet deserve the best at the end of a day. Use any lightweight shoe, moccasin, or sneaker with a sole thick enough to take the edge off rocks.

There are those who will want to forgo this luxury to save

added space and weight. Once boots and socks are off, air your feet or soak them; then put on dry socks and trail boots very loosely tied. They can be comfortable, especially if the boots fit well.

Down Boots

These nylon-covered fully insulated uppers provide wonderful added comfort in a sleeping bag. They make fine camp boots when soled with ensolite and leather. Weight: about 4 ounces. Easily packed away.

Mukluks

Nylon-covered foam mukluks provide slipper comfort and excellent warmth for subfreezing hiking on snow. As a camp shoe they are heavier and more bulky than down boots, but warmer and more serviceable on the ground.

Socks

Few hikers have found anything to compare with wool socks. They offer maximum comfort, sweat absorption, and insulation. Get the best, perhaps with reinforced nylon toes and heels for longer life.

Time-tested practice advises wearing two pairs of socks, one outer of good-quality wool with an inner lightweight sock of nylon, orlon, cotton, or a woven combination of these fabrics. However, many hikers rely on a single pair of wool socks. A hiker must decide what combination suits him best.

In any case, do not buy cheap wool socks. They wear

Mukluks *(left)* and Down Boots *(right)*

poorly, get baggy, mat about the feet, and insulate badly. Moreover, the impurities in cheap wool can cause skin ir- ritation. Those allergic to wool will find excellent wear in the orlon-nylon-cotton combinations.

To get maximum foot comfort consider using a combi- nation of hydrophobic yarn in an inner sock that wicks off foot moisture to a sock of hydrophilic yarn that absorbs this moisture.

Remember to size boots with hiking socks on.

Many hikers change socks frequently during the day. Others who hike with dry feet (or during colder weather) are able to go all day without a change. The main concern is to keep feet dry and comfortable; they will suffer a lot of wear. After a change hang the damp socks on a pack and let sun- shine do its work.

On the trail it is important to wash socks as they need it. Dirty, sweat-soaked socks are of little use in insulating and absorbing sweat. Use Woolite or a mild face soap; detergents rob wool of its oils. Rinse thoroughly and lay them out to dry on a rock or bush, but not in the sun unless in a hurry. Even then, they can be tied on a pack and probably not be in direct sunlight.

Care of Feet

Assuming that a backpacker has chosen good-fitting boots and wears the right socks, there is still the most important consideration of foot care and conditioning. Feet, more than shoulders or back, take the real punishment while hiking. To reduce the chances of soreness and blisters it is best to condition the feet before taking to the trail. Breaking in new boots and foot conditioning can be synonymous. However, other assists here will be appreciated.

One of the best foot-toughening methods is exposing the feet to air. In this respect the wearing of thongs or sandals about the house is an excellent assist. Rubbing alcohol baths also help, as do long walks on the beach.

Many hikers believe that once the boots are on they should not come off until the end of the day. However, once on the trail those with tender feet will find that regular rest stops can mean the difference between sore and comfortable feet. Enjoy that rest. Shuck those boots and dunk your feet in water if it is nearby. Rub them vigorously and dunk again. Soak them for a few moments, then let them dry out in the sunshine. Change socks before starting again, perhaps after applying foot powder. Cool, dry feet are the aim. Remember that while the air temperature reads 80 degrees, the ground temperature may reach 110 degrees. This promotes blisters and sore feet.

Blisters

The slightest bad fit of boots or creased socks will generate a blister, especially on downhill hikes. And blisters do more to ruin a trip than bad weather. Aside from the extreme discomfort, they can lead to serious infections. At the first sign of a blister (even a hint of soreness) get the boot off and apply a piece of adhesive or band-aid. By far the best cover is moleskin plasters.

If a blister does develop, after all precautions, cover it immediately. When it is large and ballooned, pierce the edge and drain. If there is time, trim off the dead skin and expose the sore to air. This will harden the underskin quicker. If hiking must be continued, cover the sore with a moleskin over a gauze patch that will not stick to exposed underskin. Once at camp for the night, expose the sore and allow air to do its job while you sleep.

Consider foot conditioning and care one of the most important parts of preparation.

chapter five

Keeping Warm
And Dry

KEEPING warm and dry is essential if a backpacker wants to fully enjoy his trip. However, reactions to cold or wet are individual, and wide differences will be noted amongst people. Everyone should determine his needs and pack only the necessary items of clothing.

A discussion of the conditions that insure trail comfort is appropriate here. An understanding of body processes and needs will make subsequent conclusions in order.

The body loses heat naturally by evaporation: first by insensible perspiration (constant skin-drying) along with moisture loss through breathing, both of which cannot be stopped, and secondly by sweating, which is subject to regulation. *Caution:* avoid sweating in cold weather. Wetness in clothes will obviate their convective insulation value. An excessive and potentially dangerous heat loss will occur as the body struggles to dry out the clothing.

The body can also lose heat by other means: radiation—

when the air temperature exceeds the temperature at the outer layer of clothing because of improper insulation, conduction—when insulation is compressed to worthlessness as a body presses to a cold surface, and convection—when insulation is not present and circulating air takes away body heat.

To control these effects and maintain a constant viable temperature, the body produces heat by burning food eaten or absorbing radiant energy from heat sources like the sun or a stove. However, the sun produces little heat in cold weather and a backpacker cannot carry a stove. Moreover, the body can only produce so much heat in a certain time span. Food consumption will reinforce heat production, but this is limited. Vigorous exercise can prolong a comfort span, as with hiking or climbing, but this is temporary. A cold body itself will attempt to regulate the heat loss by reducing the heat-carrying blood supply to extremities and skin surface, but this leads to eventual frostbite.

With the above in mind it is apparent that body heat must be preserved mechanically under adverse weather conditions, as with insulation or a heat source that maintains a balance between body heat production and heat loss. Exercise, eating, and body processes will not do the job, and so adequate clothing is the mechanical assist that creates a sustaining environment. Clothing and insulation are synonymous here.

A word here about insulation. The most effective insulation known is dead air. A contained dead air space surrounding the body will insure comfort. Following is a table indicating the amount of insulation needed under the described conditions.

Temperature (in degrees Fahrenheit)	Light Work (easy hiking)	Heavy Work (climbing)
40	.8 inch	.20 inch
20	1.0 inch	.27 inch
0	1.3 inch	.35 inch
- 20	1.6 inch	.40 inch

These values will necessarily be higher when sitting around a campfire.

Clothing

In choosing clothes flexibility is the rule and quality is preferred. Decide what the worst conditions will be and pack accordingly. The head must be protected from the elements; back and shoulders must be warm and dry. To a lesser extent limbs must not suffer the discomfort of cold. Avoid the danger of frostbite.

Think in terms of several layers of clothing. Ideally, a hiker needs a layer to absorb and wick-off perspiration, a layer to keep him warm in mild temperatures, a layer to keep him comfortable in cold, and a wind-protection layer.

Cotton or nylon next to the skin is pleasing, while fine wool is not enjoyed by many. Light wool sweaters and shirts do the job in any weather other than hot. Stay clear of cotton shirts that can feel very cold once damp, especially across the back and shoulders in cold air. Heavy wool sweaters and jackets should give way to down garments for that most important outer layer of warmth. A nylon shell windbreaker or rainsuit completes weather protection.

Adjust clothing layers. Remove or don garments at the

first signs of discomfort. Regulate with cuffs, fronts, and collars, and do not wait until miserably cold or soaked with perspiration. These layers of clothing, well regulated, will most always keep you dry and cool, or warm. And wear clothing comfortably loose. It insulates best and does not constrict the circulation of blood or warm ventilating air around the body.

Get color into clothing choices. It helps photography and is a safety factor for those who hike during the hunting seasons. A colorful garment is less likely to be left when breaking camp. Dark colors have the advantage of hiding dirt.

Underclothing

Underwear must be comfortable and neither bind nor chafe. Cotton is the preferred material because it is coolest in the summer heat and feels pleasant against sensitive skin. T-shirts are excellent garments, but damp cotton can be uncomfortable. Women may prefer their underwear of knit rayon or acetate; not nylon, for it becomes too warm.

Ventilating cotton net underwear is ideal, by far the superior garment. The mesh creates a layer of still air next to the skin, insulates, ventilates, soaks up perspiration, and allows moisture to vaporize. It prevents dampening of outer clothing and provides a warm, dry feeling in heat or cold. Ventilating underwear is available in short-sleeved shirts and long pants. Worn with a T-shirt, it will be quite comfortable in sunny summer weather above or below timberline. A word of caution: ventilating underwear worn alone in the sunshine can lead to spotted but nevertheless discomforting sunburn.

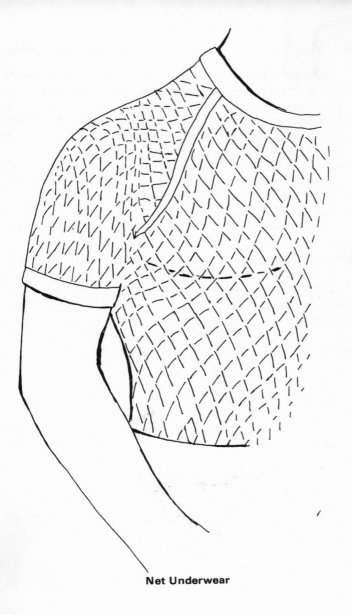

Net Underwear

The use of wool underwear versus cotton continues to be debated. Many people find wool unsatisfactory next to their skin. However, once wet it is certainly less discomforting than chilly, wet cotton. Light wool undergarments are particularly suited to cold climates or chilly nights while sleeping and, unlike cotton, wool will remain warm next to your skin when damp. It also helps evaporate insensible perspiration.

Undergarments that combine cotton and wool are also available. Two layers, cotton next to your skin and wool outside, provide the best features of both materials. These shirts and pants can be worn with ventilating underwear for maximum protection in cold weather.

Insulating underwear made with down or dacron filler is quite comfortable, though bulky. The down-filled garments cost three times as much as those of dacron, but down is the more efficient insulator. These garments should be worn with ventilating underwear to prevent perspiration from reaching them, dampening them and thereby reducing insulating values. Wash them as you would any good underwear.

Shirts and Sweaters

Shirts should have long sleeves and tails, button-down pockets, and high collars. The choice of fabrics—wool, dacron, cotton, nylon—all do the job at different times for different people.

A one-pound wool shirt is hard to beat during moderate and cold-weather hiking. Or a lightweight, close-woven wool sweater like cashmere can take the place of a wool shirt. Cotton shirts are adequate for summer use, but they can feel cold in rain or wind. Nylon is fine for cold weather; however, it does not breathe as well as wool.

Down Jackets

A wide variety of down-filled garments are available, some of them particularly suited to the backpacker. Lightweight down parkas have replaced the hiker's heavy jackets and sweaters. They are much lighter and insulate far better. Construction features like those used in down sleeping bags (see Chapter 7) are the ones to look for in a down parka.

Lightweight down creates the layer of still, dry air needed to insulate a body. It is resilient enough to crumple into a pack, yet immediately regains its loft once loose. And down will breathe, allowing body moisture to escape and maintain comfort over a wide temperature range.

For the backpacker, down jackets should weigh under 1 1/2 pounds and be considered the main body warmth preserver in his gear. Look for differential cut, a snap closure over a nylon zipper, cuffs with elastic and snaps for controlled ventilation, a drawcord hem longer than the sleeves, an attached down hood that rolls into a high down collar, large insulated pockets, and an included stuff stack.

Down Vests and Sweaters

Ultralight down vests and sweaters are warmer than heavy wool, yet lighter than cashmere. Zipper fronts, uninsulated pockets, elastic cuffs, and down collars are features of sweaters. The best vests have longer backs but seldom pockets. No hem drawcord on either of these. Vests weigh 3/4 pound and sweaters weigh 1 pound. For many, during mild summer hiking, these garments are quite adequate used with a shell wind parka.

There are those who have found that wearing an insulated underwear jacket under a rainsuit jacket can be good for a wide temperature range approaching freezing. Care must be taken to ventilate properly.

Care of Down Garments

Never keep down garments stuffed for a long time. Hang them in a dry place. Like sleeping bags, they can be sponge-cleaned for dirty spots. Machine-washing is recommended, using a mild soap and rinsing well. Dry outdoors or in a dryer at low temperatures, and be sure they are completely dry before packing.

Down Jacket Protection

During snowfall, at temperatures just below freezing, it is necessary to cover any breathing down parka with a water-proof garment. If not, the snow will melt as it touches the warm outer shell and soon you will have a useless, sodden parka. Snowfall at lower temperatures, with little body heat generating through the parka, will not be a concern. And watch out for those campfire sparks.

Combination for Comfort

A combination of ventilating underwear, T-shirt, wool shirt or sweater, and a lightweight down parka will get a backpacker through most summer hiking trips. It is important to keep the torso adequately warm and the inner organs protected. This will make extra heat available for the skin and extremities that will act as the heat radiators they should.

Pants

Trousers must be durable, able to withstand the wear and tear of rocks and brush. Get uncuffed pants that will not snag and trip you up.

Denim jeans are very tough, dark enough to hide the dirt, and easy to wash out. However, once wet they are cold and heavy. Their design can be binding in the crotch and knees when bending or kneeling.

Knickers are popular with some hikers, extremely serviceable and functional. Made of sturdy wools and cottons, these pants are warm and windproof, yet comfortable in summer. Most knickers feature double seats and knees, with a button fly usually standard. Heavier knickers of tough gabardine have leather seats sewn into them.

Orlon-rayon whipcord trail pants will provide warmth like wool when wet and are more durable. Lightweight cotton trail pants come uncuffed with generous pockets and zippered fly.

However, most knickers and trail pants are too expensive for hikers. Cheap and durable cotton work pants or jeans seem to be the most advisable.

Shorts

Shorts are definitely to be considered by the backpacker. They are light and cool, creating a rather pleasant, unconfined feeling for the hiker. Make sure they have lots of pockets, double seats, and are made of some durable material like corduroy, whipcord, or denim. Some people prefer lederhosen, but they can be warm.

While hikers may enjoy the freedom and coolness of shorts, they should remember there are disadvantages in wearing them. Sun and wind can cause severe burns for usually unexposed skin, especially at high altitudes. Insects can be a nuisance. In the brush bare legs will take a beating, while at night or dawn shorts can prove to be chilly garments. The best arrangement is to include them in any basic gear along with long pants.

Insulated Pants

For very cold-weather hiking a backpacker might consider down pants. Lightweight models have snap flies, adjustable waists, pockets, and gusseted ankles for getting them on over boots. They use sewn-through construction, and the very best designs feature outseam zippered legs, windproof outer shell, and drop seat.

Handwear

Cold-weather conditions require hand protection, hands being difficult to keep warm or get warm once they are cold. Heavy wool mittens and gloves are the favorites of many hikers. Unfortunately, gloves are not the best insulators, though they provide desired dexterity. In fact gloves actually promote heat loss. Only with 1/4 inch or better of insulation can you count on having warm fingers. However, this thickness around fingers is out of the question; so consideration must be given to insulating the fingers as a group—as in a mitten.

Heavy wool mittens are warmest, but limit the advantages of having fingers free. Extra nylon or silk liners worn with wool liners inside leather gloves will allow mittens to be taken off, say to photograph and contact metal, without fear of fingers sticking. Down-filled mittens are excellent without a liner, but be sure to have a leather palm for rough service.

Nylon-covered polyurethane foam mittens are available to keep hands warm to 0 degrees. With a nylon glove liner these will provide excellent hand protection.

Leather buckskin gloves are very durable and supple on hands; also, they dry soft after being wet. They are especially suitable for chilly summer hiking where insulation is not critical.

If covered hands become cold, remove gloves or mittens, slip your arms from your jacket, and stick those cold hands under your armpits. If the rest of you is warm it won't be long before hands are back to normal.

Headgear

The choice of hats and caps frequently seems to be decided more by whim than common sense. However, the right headgear is essential to outdoor welfare. At all times there should be head protection from wind, sun, and rain.

The head is the body's primary heat radiator. Only the head does not experience a reduction of blood supply when the body is regulating heat loss through its extremities. It follows then, as with keeping the torso warm, a head protected from the cold will allow more body heat to be distributed to the skin and extremities.

Colorful wool caps are stretchy and warm. However their snug fit can cause an itchy scalp for some. Pulled down over ears and neck, they provide good protection against cold and wind while asleep or hiking.

Wool balaclavas are more functional than caps. Folded down, they will give complete protection to ears, neck, and chin. The small visor featured in most of them is appreciated in bright sunshine or light snowfall.

A wool felt hat is practically indestructible. It is lightweight compared to caps or balaclavas, yet provides more sun and rain protection. Sit on it, carry water in it, sweep away dirt with it, or roll it into a pack without doing it much damage!

Those interested in style and tradition will consider wool berets and felt or velour alpine hats complete with colorful feathers and pins. Canvas hats with brims are extremely durable and can be dressed with feathers and pins. However, remember that these designs are limited in what they offer in protection and serviceability.

A modified stetson with floppy brim and holes in the crown can be a comfortable summer hat. It might be wise to work out a chin strap; wind can be a nuisance with these hats.

For cold weather on the slopes, or in a sleeping bag, a wool earband does good service. One advantage is the absence of pressure on the scalp as with a snug-fitting wool cap.

If very cold weather is expected, a down-filled hood, either separate or part of a parka, is advisable. Even when high winds are to be encountered, a down hood is an asset. Some are designed to completely cover neck and shoulders.

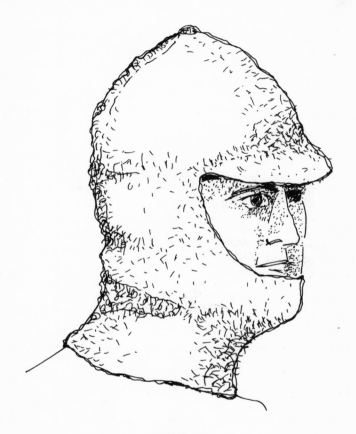

Balaclava

Deerskin Mask

Face masks are available for those weather conditions that promise frostbite. A deerskin mask is soft, windproof, and very easy to stow away.

Bandannas

Bandannas are always useful as sweat mops and sweatbands. They are good sun protection for head and neck. Soaked in a mountain stream, they provide a ready and refreshing pack against forehead or neck.

Scarf

Neck protection is sometimes forgotten by hikers until they experience discomfort that otherwise could have been avoided. It seems that this area of the body is more susceptible than any other part to rain, cold, sun, insects, and brush scratches. Balaclavas and ponchos take care of it in some instances, as do wide-brim hats and bandannas. However, some people like the feeling of a light wool scarf. In chilly weather, used with a light shirt and ventilating underwear, it can be an excellent way of getting more warmth from light clothing. Control at the neck allows regulation of the amount of heat escaping from a shirt. A scarf can also make an ideal pillow.

Raingear

No one fabric provides strength and lightness, and is wind-resistant and waterproof while being able to breathe. However, advances have been made in developing a micro-porous fabric that manufacturers maintain is 98 percent waterproof and 50 percent breathable for escaping body moisture.

An absolutely waterproof garment does not allow proper ventilation when the hiker is overheated; and trapped body moisture can be extremely uncomfortable, lead to fatigue, and even cause freezing in cold weather. Some hikers advocate breathing garments for wind and waterproof gear for rain, while others insist the best solution is the waterproof garment for both conditions. Every backpacker must make his own decision here.

Protection from rain is provided by a wide assortment of garments. Coated nylon, rubberized fabrics, and plastics are all used to manufacture waterproof parkas, rainsuits, and cagoules.

Poncho

A poncho is probably the most widely used rain garment. Generally sized from 5 by 6 feet to 5 1/2 by 7 feet, they have attached adjustable hoods with visors, snaps at wrists and sides, with grommets at the corners. They come with and without zippers. One version is designed large enough to cover a man with a pack on his back. Ponchos weigh from 1 pound to 1 1/2 pounds.

The uses for a poncho are many. It can be a groundsheet, a windbreaker, sleeping bag fly, and rain, snow, or sun shield. Two snapped together make an ideal camp shelter. A poncho can even be turned into an emergency pack slung over the shoulder. But there are drawbacks. Ponchos are bulky and tend to be a nuisance once on. They snag easily on brush and provide little leg protection. In a high wind they can prove unmanageable, even to the point of knocking you down. Moreover, if it starts to rain in camp while a poncho is doing service otherwise, either camp is upset or you get wet.

Plastic ponchos are cheap but impractical. They tear too easily, and in high winds they can become shredded in a short time. Also, the snaps are poorly made, requiring constant adjustments with a penknife. While a one-dollar investment is easily replaced, that is seldom comforting in the rain on a mountain many days' walk from a store.

Rainsuit

Waterproof rainsuits of coated nylon are very practical

garments. The jackets are made similar to wind parkas: length, draw-tight hoods, two-way zippered fronts or pull-over, adjustable cuffs, waist and bottom. Some feature pockets and visors. They weigh as little as 6 1/2 ounces.

Rain *chaps* of coated nylon weigh 5 ounces, tie to pants belt, and are not adjustable at the cuffs. However, rain *pants* usually have drawcords or elastic at the waist and cuffs.

The disadvantage with most pants and chaps is that they must be stepped into. In wet and muddy hiking the donning of rain pants can foul their insides, especially if the cuffs are elastic. One manufacturer has solved this dilemma with full zippered legs. Two-way zippers allow for ventilation adjustment, and a leather-edged cuff makes the pants more durable.

Rainsuits weigh less than a comparable poncho and do a better job of keeping you dry. The half-pound difference in weight can be counted toward a coated nylon 6 by 7 feet (8-ounce) utility sheet that takes the place of a poncho for camp use: flies, groundsheet, etc. Another small piece of plastic can be tied over a pack to keep it dry.

Cagoule

A cagoule is a cross between a rainsuit and a poncho. It looks like a pullover rain parka with extra long sleeves and a very full cut that extends well below the knees. A drawstring hem allows a hiker to pull his knees inside the garment and bivouac during a heavy rain or cold-weather mealtime. Made of waterproof coated nylon, it weighs less than a pound.

Other means of rain protection are used by many. Some

Cagoule

people rely only on sheets of plastic or lightweight tarps. Others head for the trees or rocks. And there are those who strip down in the rain, intending to dress dry and warm once the rain stops. This practice is unwise unless you are hiking in very warm temperatures during brief rain showers.

Wind Protection

One of the main reasons for body discomfort can be the loss of body heat because of wind. The importance of wind protection is indicated in the table below. It shows the correlation between the cooling effects of wind and low temperatures on exposed skin.

Wind Speed (mph)	Air Temperatures (degrees Fahrenheit)		
	30	20	10
10	16	2	- 9
15	11	- 6	- 18
20	3	- 9	- 24
25	0	- 15	- 29
30	- 2	- 18	- 33
35	- 4	- 20	- 35
40	- 4	- 22	- 36

Above 40 mph there is little increase in the cooling effect.

Wind protection is provided by many styles of jackets and parkas made of nylon or cotton or a combination of both. All of them are at least three-quarter length, equipped with draw-tight hoods, adjustable cuffs and necks, drawcord waists and bottoms. Many are double thickness at the shoulders and sleeves. The best are cotton-lined with zippered pockets and fronts, the zipper being double for opening top and bottom; overlapping facings with snap closures cover the zipper to prevent drafts. Wind parkas weigh about 1 pound; 1 1/2 pounds is tops.

Wind jackets of the pullover variety have the same features as above. However, they are not as versatile at controlling body temperatures.

Poplin wind shirts are also available, but for the backpacker they are a stylish item and weight a hiker cannot afford in his pack.

Nylon wind pants with pockets, adjustable waist and ankles can be a welcome companion to a wind jacket.

Swimsuit

While a lot of mountain hiking leads backpackers to many fine lakes and streams, few people are willing to brave the cold water. However, for those areas where the swimming is fine include a lightweight nylon swimsuit. An afternoon break and swim is a great trail refresher. In very warm weather a swimsuit can be substituted for clothing, provided one is always mindful of the sun.

Clothes Care

Underclothes and shirts, and sometimes pants, should be washed at least once a week on the trail. Socks should be washed more often. On a long trip plan on this chore for one of the layover days. Detergents are recommended for cotton and Woolite is used for wool items. However, a hand soap will do this job well. Be careful drying wool items; spread out rather than hang.

Make it a rule never to wash in streams no matter how little you think you may be contributing to pollution. Carry along a collapsible 2-gallon bucket for laundry and bathing. They weigh about 6 ounces.

Any makeshift line or bush will do for drying, although the wind may prove bothersome. Sticks and rocks will hold down items. In wet weather you are forced to the campfire or indoors to a tent, where a line strung at the ridge will serve. The close quarters with body heat will help the drying.

Extra Clothing

Always hike with an extra pair of heavy and light socks. That way, wet or sweat-soaked socks can be readily changed, and this is a good way to prevent blisters. Do the same with underwear tops and shorts. On short hikes the soiled clothing can be wrapped in a plastic laundry bag and brought back for washing. Another cotton T-shirt is sometimes good to consider. Do not forget extra handkerchiefs.

chapter six

On the Trail

THE first day out can be very important to beginners and experienced alike. What happens then tends to set the tenor of a trip. Events after are referred to it, subsequent days are better or worse, and accomplishments breed confidence for the remainder of the hike. And nothing reinforces this argument quite like an early start—as close to sunrise as possible! At least be at the trail head before the sun begins to warm backs. With gear packed and checked the night before, this is not a difficult task. Moreover, early morning is a glorious time to hit the trail: cool and fresh on summer days, or perhaps chilly enough to coax a brisk pace from everyone.

So with authorities notified, permits and maps in hand, the weather checked and satisfactory, you take to the trail.

Who Leads

Anyone can lead off a hike. With a family it is best to keep parents in front and rear, children between. Occasionally, when the going is easy, allow children to "blaze a trail." In groups the leader will often take the advance position by virtue of being familiar with the trail. His second man will bring up the rear. Keep about twenty feet apart, especially in brush. No one likes to be lashed by whipping branches, nor do those ahead like the feeling of someone on their heels. Dusty trails may require more separation, while foggy trails may call for a hand-to-pack chain. Attempt to keep up with the lead man. It is his job to keep everyone moving, perhaps even pushing them just a bit. However, if the going is too hard, ask for a change of pace. He will be accommodating. In this area special consideration sometimes must be given women and children. All too often a man's stride will quickly outdistance his family or shorter companions.

Pace

There are those who walk with goals uppermost in their mind; so many miles hiked per day is necessary for them to feel satisfied with their outing. Their rests are infrequent and their pace is brisk. Others stroll leisurely or even dawdle, sometimes to the point where on subsequent days mileage must be made up if arrival schedules are to be met. These people generally spend more time fishing, photographing, and just plain gazing at their surrounds. It is a moot question which group gets the most from their adventure; both are doing it as they see fit.

Probably a happy medium here will satisfy most back-packers: a steady pace that takes them deep into the wilderness yet allows time for leisure activities.

But in order to accomplish modest objectives and cover six or eight miles per day, it is best to consider adopting a pace with a rhythm that is reflex and not easily interrupted. Over level ground the mileage will pass quickly, if not effortlessly, once the rhythm is established and muscles are toned up. Uphill climbing will be easier and downhill passages safer.

Resting

Do not hesitate to stop to appreciate a vista or study wild flowers; this is fulfilling one of the reasons for backpacking. However, limit full rest stops to every hour. At that time get the pack off, sit and relax—feet up preferably, back against a pack propped to a rock or tree. Take off your boots and soak those tired feet in a stream. A few minutes like this every hour are revitalizing; wonderful moments that everyone looks forward to during a hike.

Other rest stops may be forced, especially on steep trails that warrant frequent stops dictated mainly by loss of wind and fatigue. Sometimes these stops will come as often as every few hundred feet. Take them; you are not on a marathon.

Hiking with a Pack

Carrying twenty pounds or more on a packframe requires special consideration for the hiker. Keep from bending forward too much. Keep an even footing and guard against placing too much weight on one leg, especially when stepping up or down in a turn where balance can be lost and the compensating strain lead to a wrenched knee. Too much of this and the knee is soon quite weak and unable to continue without great effort and pain.

Also keep from bending forward when climbing. Use steady, even steps. Let the legs do the walking, not arms and back.

On a downhill trail be careful again about bending forward. This will promote a faster, more dangerous pace. The working strain on thigh muscles increases, as does the thudding pressure on knee joints as an attempt is made to "hold back." And remember that here the blisters really mushroom. Feet are constantly slipping in boots, and toes are jammed into the boot toe. Moreover, speed here can cause a misstep on a rock that will twist an ankle and send you sprawling to an even worse injury. Caution is the word on any downhill trail.

Trail Courtesy

There is such a thing as trail courtesy, all of it based pretty much on common sense. Always consider the other backpackers, regardless of their behavior. Be a *defensive* hiker who is ready to use patience and good judgment. On heavily used trails be ready to stand aside for those hiking faster. In overtaking others be patient; most hikers will stand aside once they are aware of someone behind them. For those inconsiderates who refuse to acknowledge a passer, call ahead loudly: "Coming through!" Do not attempt to crowd by; accidents occur this way when someone is jostled off balance with a heavy pack. On the way uphill stand aside for those coming down. Take a rest then. Stand off the trail for pack animals— on the outside if standing on the inside will crowd the animals. When with a group give a hand or shove to those needing it on steep climbs.

Trail Safety

Following trail courtesy will naturally reinforce good trail safety habits. While most trails offer good footing, easy going will not always be encountered. Trails change, especially after spring thaws and storms. If the trail is obviously hazardous, stop and reconnoiter. Evaluate and discuss. Check alternate routes. If necessary, one man should attempt to negotiate the questionable trail section or alternate route. Only after it is approved will the others follow in his footsteps.

Do not hurry over stream crossings, snowfields, or rock fields. A slip from a boulder can mean a broken ankle, while a slide from a snowbound trail can mean death on rocks forty feet below.

Do not jump with a heavy pack. If need be, take it off and swing it ahead, over, up or down.

Never run, even downhill where it seems easy. A trip can be disastrous. Moreover, this is how blisters occur rapidly.

Assist anyone who needs it. Inquire if a situation seems to warrant it; most people are reluctant to ask for help, even with minor illness or blisters. Offer help even if it is obvious they are suffering because of their own miscalculation or negligence. Remember that there are usually many miles and days between help. If assistance rendered requires surrendering personal gear, then a value judgment must be made. Your own safety is paramount, but perhaps the well-being of another will mean only a passing discomfort to you.

Remember that safety is rooted in caution and routine. Impatience destroys this order. Carelessness is the result. Disaster can be the end product. Time is what there is usually plenty of. A few moments taken for safety's sake can be worth a life.

Lightning

Ordinarily there is little chance of being struck by lightning while backpacking. However, it is something to be concerned about when hiking on mountains. As chance is the biggest factor in incidents of this kind, precautions are best.

Watch the weather. Threatening thunderstorms almost always are accompanied by lightning at high altitudes. Get off ridges and peaks. Stay out from under rock ledges and caves. Travel over gentle slopes, not steep inclines. Do not seek protection from a single tree or rock taller than others. As soon as possible leave the open and get in amongst trees and brush.

When caught in the open, crouch low on your feet or sit on a pack or foam pad. Try to be the lowest object around.

Keeping on the Trail

Rely on maps and a compass and there is little chance of becoming lost. If it is obvious the trail is no longer the right one, or that you are lost, retrace steps to the point where the mistake was made. If this fails, do not panic. Sit and rethink. If necessary set up camp to spend the night. Short hikes out from this base camp will certainly cross the lost trail.

Comfort Considerations

Always try to hike in comfort. Make frequent adjustments to clothing. Do not wait until perspiration makes clothes soggy, or a chill wind causes the shivers. Button or unbutton, loosen or roll up to keep comfortable.

Keep things from slapping against waist and thighs. They can chafe an irritating sore under clothing. And do not allow gear to hang loose from a pack. In the brush this is a dangerous practice; things can catch on the branches and pull you off balance. Loose and noisy gear can be annoying to companions. Secure everything in a pack. The one exception to this might be binoculars, usually needed quickly. Heavy rubber bands will keep them in place on a pack frame.

Water

Most trails lead past water at some point. However, except in remote areas, much of the water must be considered unfit to drink. If in doubt about the water supply, purify! Purification tablets will do the job, usually in twenty minutes. The water may not look the best but it will be quite palatable. Shaking and leaving it to stand enhances the flavor of most treated water. Better still, flavor it with tea or fruit drink. Most drugstores carry purification tablets.

Boiling water for about ten minutes will also make it acceptable, although tepid water is not very appetizing.

If water is known to be scarce along the trail, an adequate supply must be carried. Rationing may be necessary to allow for needs, yet not require the carrying of excessive weights. In this case special care will be needed in designing menus that require a minimum of water. When drinking from a limited water supply, drink frequently but sparingly. Swill it in your mouth and swallow slowly. This will do a better job of thirst-quenching and reduce the tendency to guzzle what there is not much of.

Metal canteens have been the customary water carriers, but now the lighter plastic containers are finding favor. Some are collapsible. And others have waterproof caps, although these are not always reliable.

On a day hike try wrapping a canteen of ice water in newspaper. Stow it in a pack with a lunch and enjoy cold drinking water later.

Policing

Litter is and always will be a problem in our outdoor recreation areas. Witness the gathering debris at heavily used trails and trail shelters, or the horseback rangers headed along the trail with bulging trash sacks for saddle bags. Consider it a necessary chore to police trails, streams, and lakes. In wilderness areas destroy campfire sites left conspicuous. If possible remove downed trees from trails, replace fallen signs, and flag obvious route changes and dangerous conditions. Stoop to clean. Pick up trail trash and pocket it until the evening campfire. On the following morning take the time to insure that there is little evidence of a campsite. Do not leave rocks piled for a fireplace. This only encourages others to camp *exactly* in the same place.

Sanitation

It is essential that all backpackers properly dispose of human waste. Heavy use areas sometimes provide toilets. Use them only. Group backpacking will require the digging of a deep latrine, disinfectants, and lime. Two or three hikers in a wilderness area will want to copy cats and dig a private latrine. Be sure to choose a spot that will not likely be used as a campsite. Stay away from water, caves, rock ledges or clear places between large trees. Probably the more inaccessible the spot the better. Scrape a hole with a staff or boot heel, and go deep enough. Carry matches. Fire the soiled paper and cover completely with earth. When urinating take the same pains to find an area that seems quite impossible to be used as a campsite.

Discomforts on the Trail

Few hikes are completed without experiencing inconveniences and discomforts. Once back home a backpacker's tales of hardship describe situations both comic and, at the time, serious. However, most events are related with humor. Reflection and hindsight have a way of ignoring the mistakes and bad judgment that fortunately did not lead to discomforts that could not be endured.

Weather Discomfort

Weather can make or break a backpacking trip, though much of the disappointment depends on the attitude of the hiker. Rain and cold are as much a part of backpacking as fair-weather days. Accept it all.

Beautiful sunshiny days harbor the danger of sunburn. Sunglasses and hats are in order at high altitudes, especially above timberline, where sun rays cause burns more easily.

Suntan lotion will protect exposed skin, and some people will need lip cream.

Wind, too, can be troublesome. At high altitudes winds promote moisture evaporation; so hike with adequate water supply on trails where water is scarce. Salt tablets are desirable under these conditions. Without adequate precautions a day of sun and wind can be very fatiguing.

Altitude Sickness

High altitudes are frequently the cause of another discomfort experienced by those not fully acclimated to higher elevations. Since most of our population lives below 1000 feet, this is a common complaint. Headache and nausea are the usual symptoms. Aspirin and a good night of sleep are the remedies if you must start your hike without a couple of days to become acclimatized at a base camp.

Strains and Sprains

Next to blisters the most common hiker's ailment is strained muscles with their painful cramps. These are usually the result of not getting in shape before the hike. Hot baths on the trail are out, so do the next best thing: keep warm, relax, and take aspirin before turning in at night. Salt tablets can help here. On a long hike severe cramps may require a day's layover.

Hard on the heels of blisters and strains are ankle and knee sprains, usually the result of carelessness. Wrap the sprain immediately with an ace bandage and use cold applications the first day. Next day switch to heat and gentle massage.

Frostbite

To combat frostbite, always a possibility in spring or fall at high altitudes, keep clothing loose to promote circulation. During freezing weather keep a check on exposed hands and face. At the first sign of pain, numbness, or white patches on the skin, warm the area and rub *very* gently to restore circulation. Remember that damp socks promote frostbite.

Insects

At times of the year in certain areas of our country flies and mosquitoes are nearly the death of hikers. Plan a backpacking trip accordingly. Insect repellents bring relief, but seldom for long. Moreover, there is a danger of too much repellent causing skin irritation for some people. Standing around a smoking campfire helps but this can be hard on the eyes. Sometimes it will be necessary to bundle up tight and just slap away.

Other insects can cause more than just a passing discomfort. Frequently wood ticks become unwanted trail companions. In the spring and early summer they are easily picked up as hikers work through brush and grass. Check each night for signs of them, but do not touch. Crushing or pulling on them will allow the virus on their bodies to contact your skin and infect. On the trail use a heated needle, match, or taper put to its rear end; it will eventually back out. Covering them with oil or cream will have the same effect and will not risk skin injury. Wash the area with soap and water.

There is also a tiny red mite in Florida called a chigger that attaches itself to humans and sucks blood. Invariably its bite appears at the ankles, waist, or crotch, where clothing fits tightly. The bite can cause mildly painful swelling of the lymph glands, but more often it results in a maddening itchy red spot that lasts for many days, mainly because of a constant scratching for relief. "Home" remedies say this irritation can be lessened by the quick application of ice water or clear nail polish. Science claims there is little to be done. Prevent them getting to you by spraying cuffs with insect repellent.

Snakebite

The chances of encountering a poisonous snake on the trail are very slim. On the average, fewer than 2500 people are bitten each year, and seldom more than two dozen die from the bites; most of these are people with bad hearts and small children unable to combat the venom.

Of most concern to backpackers are the pit vipers (rattlesnakes, copperheads, and water moccasins) that range over most of our nation. However, their danger is more imagined than real. Fear of them is foolishly unreasonable. A little care will reduce any chance of being bitten to almost zero.

However snakebite kits should be carried. Be familiar with the instructions for quick application if necessary. When help is miles away, and expert medical attention is out of the question, have the victim rest in a cool spot. Make him comfortable and immobilize the bitten area. Continue the suction treatment for another hour, keep the wound cold with stream water or snow packs, and prepare the patient for two days of fever and nausea. Remember that few healthy people die from a *treated* snakebite.

Animals

For the most part if animals are left alone they will be of little bother. Day or night varmints can damage an unprotected food supply at an unattended base camp, but a few precautions will rid this danger. Package all food; get everything clean and packed away so as not to tempt these animals.

Bears are the only serious nuisance at any time. They are dangerous and unpredictable. Keep clear of them! Hang food high. Never take it into the tent at night. A clean camp is necessary in bear country.

For maximum protection in bear country take along para-dichlorobenzene crystals (moth crystals). One pound will do for three to five days. Keep it in an airtight plastic jar and expose it at night. This is the only proven method of keeping bears out of camp. A small sack hung outside a pack will insure protection while hiking. The smell is something else.

First Aid

Trail first aid must necessarily be an immediate application that will need to suffice, in most cases, for at least two days—until steps are retraced or objective reached and further help is available. Even in the most serious cases it may take many hours to transport an injured backpacker from the trail to medical aid. Therefore every backpacker should be aware of the need for caution and what to do for an emergency illness or injury.

Best practice is to have in the family or group a backpacker who is trained in first aid. In lieu of this get a basic first aid information sheet from a local Red Cross chapter office. Be familiar with it.

The Serious Injury

If someone is injured beyond the help of simple first aid, do not move him. Make him comfortable and warm. This is essential. Then send for help. If there are only two hiking together, leave the victim only after preparing protection and marking the area with bright-colored clothing or gear that can be seen from the air. With the site fixed in your mind, move back along the trail until you meet someone who can be enlisted to go for help or stay with the victim. Use any emergency signals available to attract attention. Contact a ranger station or sheriff's office and direct a rescue team to the victim.

Tetanus Shots

Seldom are backpackers faced with situations that will be classed as emergencies. However, minor incidents can become troublesome and eventually serious if simple safety rules are not followed. One of the simplest precautions is immunization against tetanus (lockjaw) before the trip starts. By far the greatest number of mishaps occur as blisters, cuts, and scrapes that can lead to serious infections when not attended to properly.

Treating Cuts

Contrary to common belief, cuts and scrapes do not require antiseptics that actually destroy tissue and promote further infection. Wash the cut with soap and water, dry it thoroughly, and apply an absorbent tissue and gauze pad. Resist using ointments unless a wound is already infected.

A gaping cut can be well cleaned and then pulled together with a butterfly tape bandage. In cuts of areas that get a lot of movement (knees, fingers, feet) a Steri-strip skin closure may be necessary. This application is not a difficult task. The family doctor will gladly furnish instructions once he understands the necessity for the information.

Remember that a tourniquet should not be used. Rely on pressure to stem blood flow. This technique is described adequately in first aid manuals. Study it.

First Aid Kit

A first aid kit can be quite simple for overnight trips (aspirin, adhesive, gauze pads). However, when plans are made to stay on the trail more than two days, consideration must be given to the fact that any relief in case of emergency is usually a long way off. A basic first aid kit should be designed with this in mind.

> ¼-inch adhesive roll
> 12 gauze compresses
> 12 band-aids
>   antibiotic ointment
> 12 aspirin or buffered aspirin
> 1 ace bandage
>   Steri-strip skin closures
>   moleskin patches
>   scissors

In addition are these drugs that will help insure your welfare:

codeine with aspirin (for severe pain relief or diarrhea)
tetracycline (for infections resulting in fever)
Pyridium (for bladder irritations)
Tridol (for nausea, vomiting, or intestinal cramps)
antibiotic eyedrop mixture

A family doctor will prescribe and furnish instructions as to use and dosage.

Also to be included in this list are things such as:

suntan lotion
lip cream
insect repellent
water purification tablets
snakebite kit
whistle
mirror

Trail Recreation

Getting the most out of a backpacking trip means more than just adding up the miles covered or the passes crossed. Recreation is desirable and should embrace just about whatever is of interest and enjoyment in an outdoor environment. For a start take the time to study guidebooks and maps beyond the trail information needed. Look for landscape features such as streams, springs, and peaks. Relate to them. Paying such attention tends to slow the pace somewhat, but it certainly provides a more intimate contact with the surroundings. And few backpackers are not better off for the extra moments spent in leisurely study of birds or wild flowers.

Fishing

It would be difficult to find two sports more compatible than backpacking and fishing. Few trails do not lead to water, and a day's walk will usually bring a hiker to a seldom visited lake or stream waiting to be fished. For many it is impossible to resist the lure, and fishing tackle becomes a main pack item. For these lucky few their gear is often quite simple: hooks, sinkers, flies in a 35-mm film can. Lures, leader, and bobber round out the tackle list. Nylon line wrapped around a stick is ready for a field-cut switch. Others carry separating rods and reels for spin- and fly-casting. They break down to about 20 inches and easily pack away into a pack bag. Weight: about 1½ pounds for spinning rod, reel, and tackle. A fly-casting outfit is lighter.

Books

Worth their extra weight are books that can make a hike more interesting. Interpretive books on flora and fauna, geology, and astronomy can lend a greater appreciation of outdoor involvement. Do not take all of them, but consider exploring one area on each trip. Some backpackers include light reading for late afternoon when camp is made. However, generally there is not time, what with meal and camp preparation, fishing, or just exploring.

Binoculars

There is no doubt that binoculars can enrich any hike. Numerous opportunities will occur for closer study of animal life or distant mountain ranges. Binoculars will help spot trail-blazes across a field or provide a more intimate knowledge of the surrounding countryside. Those 7 X 35 are quite adequate. Get as light a pair as possible, under 1 pound. Center focusing is best for bird-watching and close-range changes. Carry them out of the case and handy. Forget about their abuse; they are quite rugged. To keep down the weight, consider only one pair of glasses in a party.

Photography

Most backpackers want a record of their outdoor adventures, especially so of those first trips. However, camera equipment is most often costly, heavy, and elaborate. Tripod, lens, and film can bring the weight of an outfit to three pounds. Two cameras or cartridge loading are necessary when pictures are wanted in both color and black and white.

The choice of a camera is strictly personal, but it is advisable to stick with still photography. Do not discount the very cheap and lightweight instant-loading 126 cameras. They take excellent pictures, considering the limited investment.

Choose one kind of film, become familiar with it, and rely on it. Keep fresh and exposed film protected from high temperatures and humidity. Film will easily be ruined in a pack that becomes very warm with sunlight beating on it. Put exposed film into metal containers stowed in insulated bags of the type in which ice cream is often packed. These are bulky bags but they can be cut to size for two or three rolls of film. Pack this bag in the center of a pack.

Experienced backpackers often leave cameras behind, unless there is a desire to record some expected unique encounter. They recognize that photographs are seldom reviewed once developed and filed. They are also aware of the tyranny of photography. Constant evaluation of scenes, composition adjustments, light checks, camera manipulations, etc. can prevent one seeing the forest for the trees. Once rid of such considerations, there is the freedom to gaze and contemplate, to savor the environment in a way much more meaningful to many.

Writing Material

Carry along a small pocket-size notebook to record impressions, temperatures, and addresses of new friends met on the trail, or to leave messages or sketch scenes. In a pinch use the paper to start a fire. Use a pencil; ball points can bleed when too hot.

No Radio

One thing not needed in any pack is a radio; not for weather checks or otherwise. Leave it behind and learn upon returning just how little the world has changed.

chapter seven

Nights
On the Trail

WHEN to stop for the night is a matter of preference. Often a particular setting will determine a stop a half-hour before planned. Other times the necessity to have a suitable or authorized place will require another hour's hiking. Occasionally mileage requirements dictate campsite locations on the trail. Try to camp where others have not, unless designated areas must be used.

Since most summer backpacking trips will be taken during daylight-saving time, the backpacker can spend a rather long day on the trail. Not all will want to do this. Some will want to make an early stop, take a nap, and perhaps do some angling before supper.

Most camps can be set up in an hour; but selecting a campsite, collecting enough firewood for the night and morning, pitching a tent, and doing the cooking should be done in daylight for convenience.

Selecting the right campsite is an important decision, and

many factors are to be considered. Perhaps most important of these is that the site must be level and well drained. Sleeping on a slope is a tiring annoyance—even the slightest slope! If it must be endured, make sure feet are down.

In bad weather seek wind protection, especially if a tent is not to be used. Wind will drastically reduce the comfort range of equipment. Get in amongst trees and brush or rocks. The dryest place will be under a large tree or a rock ledge, but not alone and high enough to attract lightning.

Stay away from the middle of a meadow. They are usually damp and cold at night. Frost and dew invariably settle in meadows. Locate on the edge of it amongst trees or rocks.

Plan to have a water source nearby. This makes dishwashing and bathing more convenient. Moreover, the sound of running water is pleasant to some. Be sure to camp high enough above a stream so that any flash flood will not be a hazard.

Early morning starters will appreciate a campsite situated to be warmed by the next day's first sunshine.

Of major consideration, too, is the aesthetic value of a campsite choice. A shore camp overlooking a reflecting lake blanketed with ground fog, or an alpine meadow surrounded by leaden peaks silhouetted in sunset is immeasurably pleasing. Experiences like this create the stimulus for further trips into the wilderness.

Shelter

As in other areas of backpacking there exists a continuing debate over the merits of tent versus tentless sleeping. For many the thought of not sleeping with the stars for a roof is an admission of weakness. For others the security of a tent seems the more practical solution to combating fickle weather and her surprises. There are advantages and disadvantages for both methods. Remember that at best sleeping on the trail is nothing like spending nights at home.

Tentless Camping

Tentless sleeping implies a certain faith in the weather signs or a disregard for them, whatever they are. However, while gambling on the absence of rain can be successful, it is not so with gambling against frost, especially in mountain meadows. Many backpackers have to delay early starts while they dry out sleeping bags before a morning campfire. And if rain does come during the night, seldom is it not accompanied by winds that render a fly useless while you grope about in the dark with a flashlight trying to rig some protection. You are utterly lost in a downpour.

Tentless sleeping requires a combination of groundsheet and fly as a minimum to combat weather changes. Their combined weight (three pounds) is almost that of a good waterproof two-man tent at four pounds.

Unlike a tent that will raise the outside temperature by 10 to 20 degrees, especially if the wind is not blowing strong, a fly will only slightly increase the temperature range of a sleeping bag, and the air must be still.

Perhaps the best arrangement is somewhere between: tentless sleeping for those glorious summer nights or sure-dry weather; a tent when wind and rain are in the offing. However, this requires a hiker to pack both tent and groundsheet-fly combination.

An almost ideal situation arises when either can be done without, as when one hikes a trail with shelters spotted along its length. However this, too, is limiting: neighbors must be endured.

Lean-to Fly and Fire

For some the night shelter and warmth of a reflecting campfire is enough. Built against rocks or logs opposite a lean-to fly, this fire will be very much like a reflector oven: quite comfortable on a cold night. It will require periodic attention, but being half-awake at this time of night is quite pleasant when the stars are out and the air still. In the morning there will be coals for breakfast cooking.

There was a time when these lean-tos were erected with cut brush and boughs. This technique can no longer be considered; moreover, there is no need what with lightweight flies, plastics, lines, and poles.

Plastic

Sheets of plastic are cheap and quite durable when at least .004 inch thick. Just about any size desired can be had from a sporting goods store or building supply store. It costs pennies a square foot and is lightweight enough: 6 by 8 feet weighs 1 pound. Be sure to purchase translucent or opaque plastic so it can double as a sunshade.

Plastic sheets can do service as gear or tent protection, wet seats, tablecloths, water bags, drying tables, etc. They make excellent groundsheets and kitchen extensions to a tent.

These plastic sheets are quick to set up. Thrown over the shoulders, they make a ready shelter for lunch or a hiking rest during rain. In a sudden downpour they can be wrapped about body and gear, and be quite dry and warm. Be sure to allow plenty of ventilation.

Attachments

With a warning of inclement weather plastic sheets can easily be set up as shelters with the aid of nylon cord and plastic stick-on grommets. Another easy attachment for securing plastic is a keyhole-shaped wire and rubber ball device known as a Visklamp. It is a very flexible gadget, though it tends to be a nuisance; the rubber ball seems to get away from you at the most inopportune moments.

With planning, a variety of shelters can be fashioned with plastic sheets: ridge tent, wall tent, pyramid. However, the material punctures easily, and punctures lead to rips, especially in windy situations where a plastic tarp can be shredded in short time. While they are certainly expendable items, that is of little consolation when suddenly without one. A hiker should not rely on plastics for long trips where replacement is impossible short of carrying two sheets. If it is to be used, a heavy thickness of .006 inches might prove best in high winds encountered on mountaintops or prairie trails.

Plastic Tube

Plastic tubes make excellent shelters. These, too, are lightweight and cheap, providing roof and groundsheet in one. Only a length of nylon cord is needed to rig a ridge support between two trees. Gear will spread the tube out on the ground. Tube dimensions are 9 feet in circumference and 9½ feet long. A two-man model is 12 feet in circumference. Some have grommets at the ends for closing. The smaller tube weighs about 1 pound, while the larger weighs about 1½ pounds.

Nylon Flies

Nylon flies are available in a variety of sizes. They are usually coated waterproof nylon with several grommets located around the edges and equispaced on the surface of the sheet. A 5 by 7 foot fly will weigh less than a pound.

In conjunction with nylon cord, trees, or tent-pole arrangements, nylon flies can provide a fairly dry camp. However, while a fly may be set to ward off wind and rain from one direction, a sudden change in direction can be drenching before there is a chance to adjust the fly. One solution is to arrange the fly with a low ridge and sides close to the ground. Although this may be cramped it will be dryer. A groundsheet and ditching will take care of seepage and runoff.

Groundsheets

While coated nylon tarps are more durable, a plastic sheet is the best material for this job. Plastic costs a fraction of what a nylon tarp costs. Groundsheets protect nylon articles from rough ground abuse (under a sleeping bag or seat) and they keep you dry and clean. They make good sense under a tent floor. When sleeping under the stars and waking to a light rain, it is a simple matter to roll up in the groundsheet. It will at least protect the bag while a fly or poncho is rigged for shelter.

Poncho

As with plastic sheets and nylon flies, a poncho can be strung to make an adequate shelter from wind, rain, and sun. Yet none of these materials or arrangements provides the weather protection of a tent.

Tents

Ideally a backpacking tent should be light, waterproof, durable, insect-proof and low-cost. It should be large enough for its occupants and their equipment. However, it is not to be considered the roomy enclosure of a campground tent, for only nighttime and the most inclement weather drives a backpacker under shelter. Moreover the nature of hiking (covering predetermined mileage with limited food supplies) requires a hiker to move on through the weather while forgoing the luxury of rainy days spent snug in a roomy tent.

Tent Materials

High-count cotton fabric and nylon are the two fabrics usually found in the construction of good lightweight tents for backpackers. Treated cotton fabrics weighing at least six ounces per square yard will provide excellent water-repellent shelter. It will be rot- and mildew-resistant, while still being able to breathe. There will be little frost buildup inside a cotton tent in cold weather.

The universal material for lightweight tents is ripstop nylon, either treated for water repellency or coated to be waterproof. Nylon and dacron threads are used along with nylon zippers and aluminum poles.

Tent Construction

Look for tents featuring lap seams sewn double, catenary cut to eliminate sag, coated waterproof sides and floors of one piece, reinforcing at strain points, grommets or braided nylon tape loops, sleeves for poles, and adequate screen doors and vents that can be opened from inside or outside. Number 7 nylon zippers are adequate.

Poles are aluminum and sectional for easy packing. Shock-cord sectioned poles that are self-erecting will prove very practical.

Other features to look for are zippered cookholes in the tent floor and covered vestibules extending from the tent's front door.

Tent Designs

There are several basic tent designs, determined mainly by the number of occupants. A ridge type, with rectangular floor and short walls, is the customary design for one- and two-man tents. One-man tents often have rear-sloping ridges and rear-narrowing floors, while some tents feature side pullouts to insure more inside space.

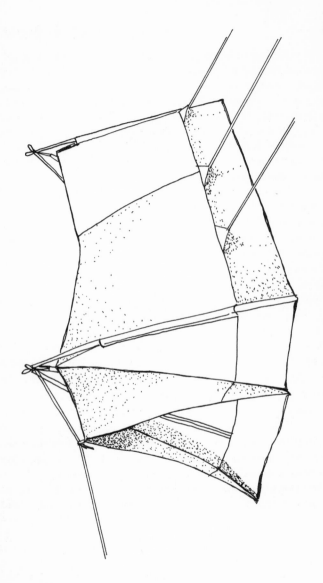

Ridge Tent

One-man tents, weighing less than three pounds, barely allow enough room for a packer and his gear unless they are equipped with a vestibule for storing gear. If long indoor stays are anticipated, a hiker should consider the roominess of a two-man tent. For two people these tents are adequate. A 4½ by 7½ foot tent weighs from 4 to 6 pounds and provides enough room for gear.

A pyramidal-type tent with a square or hexagonal floor is used for three men and more. It will weigh from 8 to 12 pounds, but this weight is distributed at an average of 3 pounds per hiker—that of a one-man tent.

Other models double as a closed, secure tent for one, but can be opened up to provide roof shelter for three in tentless camping. These are very lightweight (under two pounds) and inexpensive.

Most nylon and cotton tents must use waterproof flies during heavy rains. Strung a few inches above the tent roof, these flies provide excellent weather cover, and are good insulators if the tent is to stand in sunshine.

Doing away with the expense and weight of a fly, one manufacturer provides a 4 by 7 foot tent made entirely of waterproof nylon. Continuous screen ventilation is provided around the tent wall under the eaves. Tapes close off wind and rain whenever necessary. Condensation is minimal, especially if the tent is pitched under brush or trees away from dew and frost areas. These tents weigh under 4 pounds and are roomy enough for two packers and their gear. Their dimensions when packed are 4 by 8 by 12 inches.

The same manufacturer has developed another similar tent of coated nylon with an applied layer of foam inside

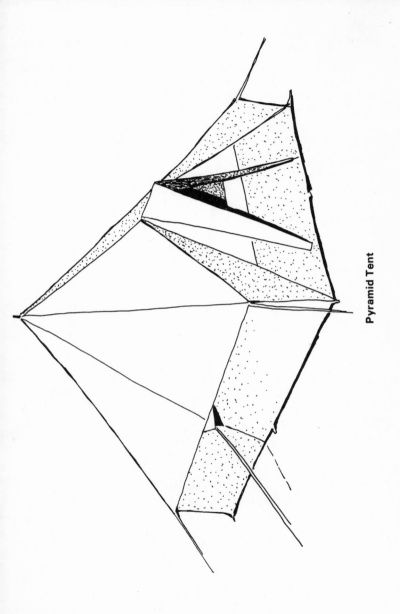

Pyramid Tent

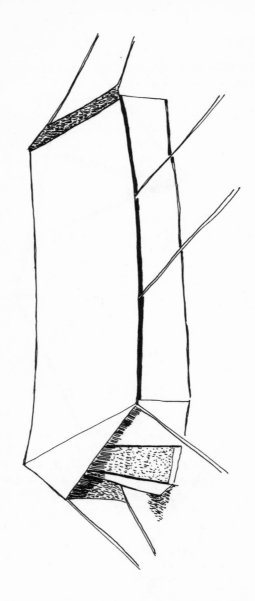

Waterproof Two-Man Tent

designed to do away with condensation altogether and provide some thermal insulation.

Tent Poles and Pegs

Few lightweight tents are designed to be pitched without poles and pegs, although most can be erected without them. When hiking in timber a place to string a ridge line is not difficult to find. However, better take along those poles when headed above the tree line.

Aluminum poles are sectional and seldom over two feet long when broken down. Some are self-erecting with shock-cord interiors. Sectional fiber glass wands can be purchased and used to take the sag out of tent walls.

A variety of metal pegs are available. Wire pegs or nails are convenient and lightweight. In dirt too soft or hard, rely on rocks or logs to hold down line tied to the pegs. Wood pegs can be cut and fashioned, but are not worth it, considering the weight of a hatchet that will be needed. A peg-pole set will weigh from 1 to 1½ pounds for most two-man tents.

Tent Care

Most tents are durable enough to provide years of service if certain commonsense procedures are followed. Extreme care should be taken when cooking in a tent. Fill the stove and light it outside. Store gear carefully so as not to puncture the tent floor. Never wear boots inside a tent. Keep it clean: sweep out the dirt before packing it up in the morning. Machine-wash it when necessary. Use a mild soap, rinse well, and spin dry. Do not leave a wet tent rolled up more than a few days. Dry it thoroughly before storing away. And take care to keep the pole set clean and easy to assemble.

Importance of Ventilation

There is a danger inherent in the use of sheltering plastics and weathertight tents. In the latter the danger occurs when ventilation is cut off, such as in a snow when drifting can take place at night while sleeping. With plastic the problem arises when the plastic is allowed to collapse around someone and form a wet bond, as plastics can easily do, either on itself or to wet dirt. Asphyxiation is the danger here. Asphyxiation is the lack of oxygen and the presence of carbon dioxide, which, fortunately, will usually warn you—even wake you. However, excessive moisture inside a shelter may absorb this warning carbon dioxide and you may never wake.

An even greater danger is from carbon monoxide, the deadly gas produced when a burning stove in a confined space uses up the free oxygen. There is no warning! Even a small can of sterno can kill.

Insure proper ventilation of shelters at all times.

Sleeping Gear

A warm, comfortable night of sleep is worth anticipating at the end of a good day's hike. Moreover, it is essential if the following day is to be enjoyed. A third of the day will be spent bedded down, and it is necessary to have comfortable sleeping gear that will preserve body warmth and insulate against cold and wind.

Accepted practices for regular camping, sleeping in blankets and heavyweight bags, will not do for backpackers. These items cannot be easily carried, nor will they provide adequate warmth at the higher elevations often encountered when backpacking.

How Much Insulation

First consider the reasons for determining the insulation needs of good sleeping gear. To be comfortable body temperature must remain at 98.6 degrees Fahrenheit. To maintain this heat, food eaten is burned up at the rate of approximately 3000 calories a day. When hiking a full day nearly 4500 calories will be needed. While relaxed at the campfire, or sleeping, about 100 calories of heat are used up per hour. In cold weather calories of heat must not be lost faster than they are produced. To accomplish this, insulation is needed. The table below indicates how much insulation is needed while sleeping.

Temperature (in degrees Fahrenheit)	Insulation (in inches)
40	1½
20	2
0	2½
-20	3

Temperatures are for still air. Wind blowing across the insulation will require greater thickness. Moreover, cold sleepers may need more insulation.

Insulation Material

Second consider the choice of material for insulation.
While dry, still air is the most effective insulation known, it
must be contained to be functional. At 20 degrees Fahrenheit,
two inches of any material that deadens air circulation will
do the job. Foam, kapok, or dacron insulate all right, but
they are too heavy. Because of a backpacker's special needs
it is necessary to use a material that will provide maximum
insulation at minimum weight. Down is that material. Down
sleeping bags are the best for insuring that good night of
sleep.

A down sleeping bag is the most expensive item in a backpacker's gear. However, it is the most important item and
care should be taken to select a proper one. This can be a
difficult job, even though it is the only type to consider.
Other types exist, but have no place in a backpacker's lightweight gear, for one pound of down is 2½ times as warm as
a pound of synthetic filling. Nevertheless, *do not judge a
sleeping bag by the weight of down in it.*

The warmth of a bag depends on several factors: quality,
amount, and loft of down; shape of bag, temperatures, wind
exposure, dampness, individual metabolism, physical conditioning, and clothing. A discussion of these characteristics
follows.

Nylon is the basic covering material of modern sleeping
bags. Many times stronger than any other readily available
cloth of the same weight, it is durable and allows easy movement within the bag. Nylon breathes well and dries quickly.

Down is the principal bag filler, of which there are many

grades. The very best white prime northern goose down will fill 500 to 600 cubic inches per ounce of down; yet it is resilient, compressing to 15 cubic inches for packing. Upon unpacking, it will readily regain its original loft. Gray goose down is inferior to white goose down, while white duck down is inferior to gray goose down (fills 400 to 500 cubic inches per ounce). Always read the state bedding tag before buying a bag. It will tell the color and type of down. And check carefully specifications in advertisements; if a supplier does not tell about these details, there is a good chance his merchandise is inferior.

Construction

Well-made bags provide differential cut (inside shell smaller than outside cover). This feature helps retain constant bag thickness. Circumference baffles divide the bag into tubes that stop down from shifting over the bag's length. One or more baffles running from head to foot will reduce circumferential shift of down. Slant wall baffle and overlapping tube baffle construction are the two generally employed.

These inside baffles are made of nylon or netting, usually on 6-inch or 8-inch centers. Overlapping tube baffle construction provides the best down control, but adds to the weight of a bag. Bags with sewn-through seams have cold spots; their use is limited to very mild temperatures.

Fittings for liners and integral pillow closures that can save the cost of down hood, are all features of good bags. Nylon zippers are preferred. Zippers should be backed with a down-

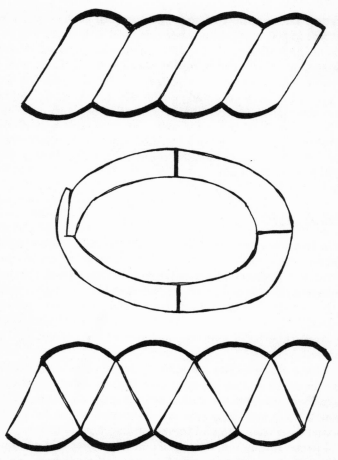

Slant Wall Baffle *(top),* **Differential Cut** *(center),* and
Overlapping Tube Baffle *(bottom)*

filled tube to insure complete insulation. Be sure the opening is taped to prevent zipper snags.

Design

There are two basic designs of sleeping bags: the mummy bag, which is the best insulator but is confining to many packers, and the rectangular bag, which allows more freedom but can be colder. Since heat loss through radiation is proportional to the surface area of a bag, the mummy will be lighter while doing the best job.

Optimum warmth and light weight are provided by bags without zippers. They are not as difficult to get into as is generally believed. However, their use is drastically limited in a broad temperature range. A full-length zippered bag is preferable.

Some manufacturers provide bags that zip together, thereby extending the cold temperature range of the bags.

Loft

Loft is the thickness of a down bag as it lies zipped up. A minimum of two inches dead air space is needed all around a body to keep it comfortable at 20 degrees Fahrenheit. The loft of a bag is an indication of comparative insulation values. Good bag design provides maximum loft with minimum weight of down. The table below is a guide to the comfortable loft a person should look for at temperatures when no wind is blowing over the bag.

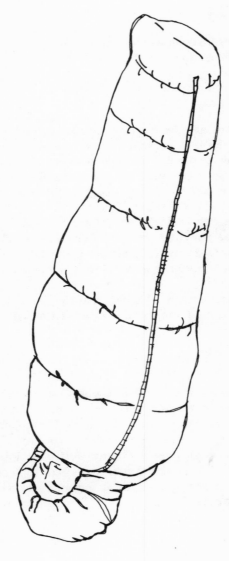

Mummy Bag

Minimum Temperature (in degrees Fahrenheit)	*Loft* (in inches)
40	4
25	5½
15	6
5	6½
- 20	8

Care

Do not dry-clean a down bag. Remove stains by spot-sponging the covering with mild soap and warm water. If necessary, hand wash it gently in mild soap and warm water. Thoroughly dry it in a dryer for several cycles at low temperatures. It can also be dried outside on a clothesline, in the sun and breeze. Make sure to fluff it occasionally. Never pack it wet.

Never leave a bag stuffed for long periods of time. For long-term storage hang it in a dry place.

On the trail unpack a bag a half-hour before using. Shake and fluff it, allowing it to recover its loft. Never use a bag without some protection under it; nylon cannot take the abuse of rocks and sticks. Do not sleep with wet clothing on; body metabolism is at its lowest and valuable calories are lost drying the wet articles. Dry damp clothing in a bag only if you are warmer than necessary and the clothing is loose in the bag. If there is an opportunity, air a bag each morning in the sun.

Sleep wearing light underclothes or nothing. Remember, the bag is a nightshirt.

Use a bag liner. Many bags are equipped with inside fastenings to accommodate liners. Some are made of nylon, others of cotton. The investment is worth it, since it is a simple matter to wash a liner.

Insulation and Comfort

A down sleeping bag will not prevent heat loss to the cold ground. Here the compressibility of down works against us. Protection is needed here. Air circulation and heat loss by convection in air mattresses make them unsatisfactory unless space in a pack is the paramount consideration. Open-cell foam pads (polyurethane) have replaced the air mattress. They are lighter and more durable. They are more efficient insulators. Moreover, they eliminate the tiring task of inflating an air mattress. Open-cell foam pads are softer-feeling than closed-cell pads; however, they require three times the thickness to provide comparable insulation value. One and a half inches of open-cell foam is a minimum for comfort and insulation, rated effective far below the temperatures a packer will ordinarily encounter.

Get a pad with its own tie cords and compartment for rolling up, or one with a stuff sack. Make sure it has a removable cover with waterproof nylon bottom. The pads have to be washed occasionally; if wet, the foam must be dried. A pad should provide comfort from the shoulders to below the knees. A 20-inch width will be adequate. A covered pad 1½ by 20 by 48 inches will weigh 1½ pounds.

Particularly hardy hikers, willing to sacrifice comfort for weight savings, use closed-cell ensolite pads. Such pads will weigh about 1 pound and measure 3/8 by 20 by 48 inches.

Other Considerations

The metabolism rates (heat generation) of sleepers vary widely, according to fatigue and how well fed they are. Because of these factors some people sleep hot or cold. Hence the need for a fully adjustable opening on bags.

Wind blowing over a bag will conduct heat away faster. It can also penetrate the bag somewhat and reduce the effective loft.

Bedding down in the open under the stars on a cold night will result in more heat loss due to radiation than would occur on a cloudy night or in a tent.

While our only consideration here has been of down bags, there are adequate synthetic-filled bags. They are much heavier, but machine-washable and good for children's use. Those allergic to down will also find them suitable. A family of packers might well consider the heavier synthetic bags for the necessary pack load per person is reduced because of communal use of tents, utensils, food stoves, etc.

Sleeping bags made of nylon-covered thin polyfoam are also available now. They are heavier than down bags and more bulky, yet quite a bit cheaper. These bags are excellent for very cold weather outings.

Of real importance to budget-minded families is the disposable paper sleeping bag. It costs only a few dollars. It weighs 2½ pounds, and is waterproof yet breathes to allow moisture to escape. Do not use below 40 degrees Fahrenheit.

Keep in mind that no one bag will satisfy all requirements for low altitudes and timberline freezes. Select a bag for the coldest expected use, while being sure it can be adjusted for warmer nights.

Sleeping Cover

For the packer who seeks the ultimate in lightweight packing, the sleeping cover is an answer. Using a space blanket 56 by 84 inches (layered aluminum and plastics available from most outdoor suppliers and stores), sew or grommet flannel to the hem on reflecting side. Leave an extra 12-inch flap at top to cover head. Fold bottom flannel and space blanket to make a pocket. Size pocket to sleeping length, being sure to bring flannel up as far as knees. Sew up the pocket sides. The sleeping cover is for two packers and weighs 2 pounds.

Unlike a down bag a sleeping cover does not allow evaporation of moisture through the material. However, the loose fit of a cover from knees to shoulders will allow controlled air circulation. Sleep with some clothing on to absorb insensible perspiration (continuous skin-drying body process). On dry nights the flannel liner is adequate for moisture absorption. Two people can be comfortable at 32 degrees. One person can be comfortable at 32 degrees in a modified narrower (30 x 84 in., 1½ lb.) version of the sleeping cover. A hiker using a sleeping cover in a tent and equipped with a down jacket should be able to get through any unexpected cold night while summer packing.

Depending on humidity and campsite (open fields subject to dew and frost), a sleeping cover may have to be packed damp in the morning. Take a break during the day and dry it out.

A sleeping cover requires home sewing. However, the effort and $10 cost are worth it, considering the important

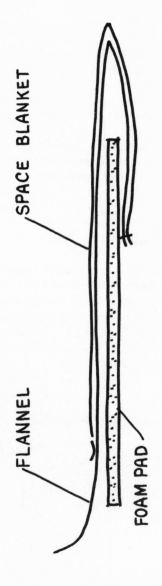

FLANNEL

SPACE BLANKET

FOAM PAD

Sleeping Cover Cross Section

weight savings. With reasonable care it will last several years. It packs to 3 by 8 by 8 inches.

Low-cost sleeping covers are especially suited to families with limited backpacking budgets. Youth groups will also appreciate this savings, and the construction of sleeping covers makes a good project.

Discretion must be used when deciding to use a sleeping cover; you do need a tent. Except in very mild weather ground drafts of cold air will make them ineffective when used without shelter.

Why a Sleeping Cover

The concept of a sleeping cover allows substantial weight and cost savings in a backpacker's basic gear. Two packers substitute a 2-pound sleeping cover for two 4-pound bags. Packframes and bags at 4 pounds each are replaced with day packs at 1½ pounds each. There is an 11-pound reduction for two people. This is what gear paring is all about. Below are comparative weights and costs.

2 Hikers w/Sleeping Cover

	Weight	Cost
1 2-man tent	4 lbs.	$ 60
1 sleeping cover	2 lbs.	10
2 day packs	3 lbs.	40
	9 lbs.	$110

2 Hikers w/Sleeping Bags

	Weight	Cost
1 2-man tent	4 lbs.	$ 60
2 sleeping bags	8 lbs.	130
2 packframes & bags	8 lbs.	60
	20 lbs.	$250

1 Hiker w/Sleeping Cover

	Weight	Cost
1 tent	3 lbs.	$ 60
1 sleeping cover	1½ lbs.	10
1 day pack	2 lbs.	25
	6½ lbs.	$ 95

1 Hiker w/Sleeping Bag

	Weight	Cost
1 tent	3 lbs.	$ 60
1 sleeping bag	4 lbs.	65
1 packframe & bag	4 lbs.	30
	11 lbs.	$155

Costs are representative of comparative equipment values. More can be spent but not less if adequate criteria are maintained.

Ideally, a backpacker will include both down bag and sleeping cover in his basic gear, utilizing them as best fits the needs of a particular trip.

Regional Requirements

Freezing weather does come to nights in Florida during December, January, and February. However, it is generally an infrequent dawn freeze, seldom more than a single day. Average winter night temperatures are in the low 50s. Foam pads can be left behind when packing in Florida. Dead grass, pine needles, or oak leaves will provide good insulation over the sandy soil. Sleeping covers are adequate for all seasons in Florida.

Temperatures seldom reach freezing in the eastern mountains during the summer months, although spring and fall can provide cold nights. Sleeping bags can be light. Sleeping covers are adequate.

More than one hiker has found himself in snow in the Tetons during the summer. Be prepared in the Rockies. Bad storms and freezing weather can overtake packers on a 4-day trip.

California weather is usually delightful, but frosty nights can follow balmy summer days. It will freeze at Lassen in July. Count on needing to keep warm at frost temperatures. Sleeping covers are adequate if you feel sure of the weather.

The Northern Cascades of Washington provide chilly summer nights. Sleeping covers are adequate, but check the weather carefully.

chapter eight

Trail Cooking

PREPARING meals on the trail is thought by some to be an exciting challenge, while others consider this a dull chore. For sure, gourmet cooking is just about impossible. However, this does not mean that wholesome and palatable meals cannot be served from a campfire.

Food Values

Much has been written about food for backpackers. Detailed analyses have been drawn up concerning proper diets, the right amounts of protein, fats, carbohydrates, etc. Calories have been discussed ad infinitum. There will be no attempt here to repeat in detail these various findings, some of them at odds. For the most part they are of little concern to a backpacker planning a trip of less than a week's duration.

When selecting food and menus keep in mind that the average person will need enough food to provide about 2500 calories a day while in camp and up to 5000 calories a day when mountain hiking with a pack. However, it is not necessary to consume enough food to provide this amount of calories each day. Stored body fat (4000 calories per pound) will take up the slack. There are few backpackers who would miss the loss of a couple of pounds.

Food Choices

How much and what to take is learned by trial and error. Often foods that are appealing at sea level are just not palatable at 10,000 feet. This is especially so of fat foods. And at higher elevations a sweet tooth and salt craving can overcome the most careful dieter. When choosing food consider that the best value is bulk, for most foods are a combination of the daily needed fats, proteins, and carbohydrates. And two pounds of food will provide this, allowing that every ounce of fat food furnishes about 200 calories while protein and carbohydrates yield about 100 calories per ounce.

An average eater can consider that 10 ounces of carbohydrates provide 1000 calories; 5 ounces of fat foods provide 1000 calories; 10 ounces of protein foods provide 1000 calories. Total: 3000 calories for 25 ounces. Anything else needed can be drawn from the body reserve.

Food Weight

Freeze-dried and dehydrated foods are the only kind to consider on a backpacking trip other than a day hike or an overnight outing. These are easy to prepare and quite palatable.

How much to take depends on individuals. Some will want 2 pounds a day, while others will get along on one pound of these prepared foods. For the most part duplicate meals at home, emphasizing fats and proteins.

Nearly all food items are now packaged for individual or double servings. Most come in plastic or aluminum containers. However, to further reduce food weight, repackage items in plastic bags to get rid of heavy cans and cardboard outer wrappers. Package portions for each meal and then contain these smaller packages in a plastic bag.

Food Preparation

Keep it simple! Use one-pot meals whenever possible. Stews and goulashes are extremely satisfying to most everyone, offering a camp cook a chance to come up with a variety of flavors. These meals will be hot, tasty, and easy to prepare.

Breakfast: consider wake-up juice, instant hot cereal with raisins and honey. Munch cookies with hot tea or coffee. Variety: pancakes, bacon and eggs.

Lunch: try more of that morning drink with a bacon bar and cheese or peanut butter crackers. Cookies make a good dessert. Variety: tuna or ham salad mix, hard salami, cheese.

Supper: concoct a stew. Drink iced tea and finish off the meal with soaked dried fruit and cookies. Variety: freeze-dried steaks, chops, whipped potatoes.

During the day drink lots of water with fruit flavors. A combination of raisins and chocolate bars makes for good snacking. This also provides an excellent energy boost on those long days when you are exposed to drying winds and sun.

Menus

Menus and food preferences are highly individual choices depending on needs, attitudes, conditions, and appetites. Everyone learns by trial and error what is best for him. Following are menus that have proven quite adequate for a healthy 190-pound man and a 130-pound woman.

Breakfast (8 oz.)
> Tang
> cereal with raisins and honey
> tea bags
> cookies

Lunch (8 oz.)
> Tang
> bacon bar
> crackers, peanut butter or cheese
> cookies

Supper (16 oz.)
> stew (noodle mix, onions, peas and carrots, meat bar)
> iced tea
> cookies
> dried fruit

Campfire Snack (5 oz.)
> hot chocolate
> cookies

Supplements (6 oz.)
   salt
   sugar
   raisins
   chocolate bars
         or
   energy sticks

These menus represent about 21 ounces per day for one person.

Of course the above meals can be supplemented by berries and nuts in season, or fish in the frying pan when fortune smiles. But do not count on either.

Food Purchases

To be sure, lightweight foods cost extra. However, this is vacation time or at least a weekend of relaxing. The weight-saving and ease of preparation is worth the money.

Most of what a backpacker will want to take along to eat can be bought in a supermarket. It is cheaper, just as tasty, and certainly more readily available at the last moment than are foods ordered from a catalog. Nevertheless, sporting goods stores and food mail order firms do have a much wider variety of lightweight items than can be found in any supermarket.

Following is a list of food that complements the previously described menus.

Item	Minimum Serving	Type	Super-market	Sports Store or Mail Order
bacon bar	2	precooked		X
cereal	1	instant	X	
chocolate bars	1	no-melt		X
cookies	1		X	
crackers	1		X	
dried fruit	1			X
energy sticks	1	concentrated	X	
honey	1			X
hot chocolate	1	instant	X	
iced tea	1	instant	X	
meat bar	2	concentrated		X
noodle mix	4		X	
onions	1	freeze-dried	X	
peanut butter	1		X	
peas and carrots	1	freeze-dried		X
raisins	1		X	
salad mixes (tuna, ham)	2	freeze-dried		X
salt	1		X	
sugar	1		X	
Tang	1	instant	X	
tea bags	1		X	

No Cooking

It is now possible to take a weekend or week-long trip and never put a match to a stove or fire. Countless food items can be eaten cold, and on warm summer days this is not at all unappetizing. Select menus from the list of foods above.

While all of this may not be as palatable as hot meals and drinks, it nevertheless does the job. This method is especially worthwhile when miles must be covered and hiking is a dawn-to-dusk outing.

First Day Treat

On the other hand, consider the consummate pleasure of eating a thick steak and baked potato at the end of that first day on the trail. Take a steak along, frozen and wrapped in a freezer bag or newspaper. A piece of foil will help bake that potato in the coals.

Perhaps one could bend a little and not worry about the extra weight on his back. The idea is certainly tempting.

Fires

Campfires and backpacking are inseparable. An open fire remains traditional, a part of the romance of being outdoors. Smells of coffee and bacon cooking on an oak fire conjure up all manner of pleasant thoughts. However, there is a distinction between a small cooking fire and those evening blazes that backpackers gather around to gaze into for hours and are quite reluctant to leave.

Cooking Fire

The cooking fire is as practical as an evening campfire is enjoyable. In the morning chill it is a welcome day-starter. Relying on a fire means there is no heavy stove gear to pack. And more than one pot can be on a fire. They are certainly quieter than stoves.

However, fires can be a nuisance. Wood must be gathered. Fires are frequently hard to start. They can smoke terribly. They must be tended and put out. This takes time away from leisure hours in camp and makes for late starts in the morning. Nevertheless, for those who maintain this is the only way to cook, these inconveniences are a small price to pay for the pleasures of savoring food with a campfire tang.

Cooking fires should be small, fueled with dead wood no thicker than a thumb. Excellent fires to brew tea or warm up soup can be made from a pencil-sized twig and debris to be found within a few feet of most campfires.

Do not build fires on humus, and keep them away from trees, brush, and downed logs. Clear a spot down to the soil and back two feet from the fire. Use rocks for a fireplace small enough to heat two pots using a grate, or span the rocks with the pots. A large flat rock can act as a sideboard.

Pile kindling in an upright position and fire. Have ample wood on hand to maintain a good blaze for cooking chores. Remember that a small fire will require more attention. To insure an easy start some backpackers carry heat tablets or igniter paste.

Light woods ignite easily but burn fast. Hardwoods are difficult to start but last longer.

Campfire

Frequently the cooking fire becomes the evening campfire. Enlarging the fireplace and adding wood is about all that is needed. However a campfire will require more vigilance. The fire is three or four times larger and that makes it more dangerous.

Do not create a blaze that you cannot stand close to. Fuel it with wood that is sure to burn in an hour's time. And add this wood carefully to prevent sparks from shooting off into the trees and grass. This will also reduce the chance of flying sparks burning nylon jackets, tents, and sleeping bags.

Grates

This is one item every kitchen should have. Although many arrangements can be made using sticks and wire hangers (even green wood will make a good grate over a small fire), a metal grate is easier and just as efficient.

A variety of grates are used: homemade wire grates, patches of expanded metal lath, and small barbeque grills. However, some of them weaken and sag over a fire. Anything stronger usually means more weight.

One answer to this is a model that features stainless steel tubing, is 5 by 15 inches and weighs only 3 ounces. This is hard to beat.

Instead of using a grate, you can pull rocks close together so that pots will span the rocks. Build a small trench fire under. This is especially efficient if a good breeze is blowing.

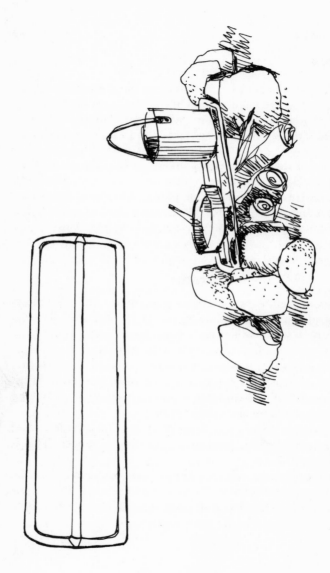

Backpacker's Grill

Stoves

Under certain conditions using a stove is the only way to prepare food. In some areas of the East and Pacific Northwest, where days of drizzling rains can make a wood fire impossible, a stove must be carried. Dry seasons and the danger of fire can require the use of a stove. If plans call for meals to be fixed above the treeline, then a stove is necessary, as when winter backpacking in snow.

Cooking with a stove saves fussing with fires, keeps pots clean, takes less time, and allows for earlier morning starts; there is no lengthy cleanup as with fires. And the advantages of being able to prepare a hot cup of coffee inside a tent in bad weather bolsters the arguments of those who would not cook any other way.

However, there is a weight and bulk problem with stoves. On a week trip a backpacker starts with about 3 pounds (stove and fuel) and ends with 1½ pounds (stove and empty fuel containers). Moreover, these small one-burner stoves can weigh anywhere from 12 ounces to 54 ounces plus fuel. They burn white gasoline or kerosene and butane or propane. Extra fuel may have to be included in a pack.

Among the different models there are advantages and disadvantages. A butane stove takes almost twice as long to boil water as does a gasoline stove. But for simplicity and convenience, for cleanliness and less weight, either a butane or propane stove is the best choice. Extra cartridges may have to be carried, but they are certainly cleaner than liquid fuel containers.

All of these small stoves have their idiosyncrasies. Look for features that include low weight complete with fuel, con-

Stoves: Gasoline *(left)*, Butane *(center)*, Propane *(right)* venience of use, stability once set on the ground, fuel capacity, burning time, extra fuel needs, and cost.

Tent Cooking

There will be a time for some backpackers when meals must be prepared in a tent. Rain and severe cold may drive you inside. Perhaps a summer blizzard will overtake you.

Fire is always a danger inside a tent, especially in those cramped quarters when using stoves that start with an uncontrollable burst of flame. If possible, set up the stove outside but close to the tent. Fire it there and then bring it in. Be sure to have all the food ready to cook.

More dangerous than fire is carbon monoxide. In a closed area a flame will quickly use up the available oxygen and create a poisonous gas that kills without warning. Insure proper ventilation.

High-Altitude Cooking

The boiling point of water falls 1 degree Centigrade with every 1000 feet rise in elevation. At sea level water boils at 100 degrees Centigrade. At 5000 feet it boils at 95 degrees Centigrade, and at 10,000 feet it boils at 90 degrees Centigrade. Add a little salt and the boiling point increases. Barometer pressure changes will raise or lower it.

Therefore, the higher a backpacker climbs the longer it will take to cook those meals that require boiled water. This is the reality, but forget its importance. Just be patient and sample the cooking food. Cooking aromas will be all the more tantalizing for the wait, and the food will be just as delicious.

Axe and Saw

Today there is no reason for either of these on a backpacking trip. Leave them at home. They are heavy and cumbersome. A rock will drive tent stakes as well as an axehead. A campfire should be small enough so as never to require wood that cannot be hand-broken. Kindling can be whittled with a jackknife.

Jackknife

This is the only cutting tool needed. It can be used in cooking (cutting up food), building a fire (shaving wood chips), equipment repair (punching holes in leather), and first aid (removing splinters). Get one with at least two blades, can opener, and punch. One to a party of two. Quality only.

Utensils

Only take what is absolutely needed. With good planning a real weight saving can be realized here. Eat from the cooking pots or frying pan. Make one item do where ordinarily two would have been used.

Complete kitchen for two:

> grate
> 2 1-qt. pots nesting with lids
> frying pan (teflon-coated pie pan)
> pot holder
> 2 thermal bowls
> 2 cups
> 2 spoons

   pint plastic container (watertight lid)
   jackknife
   collapsible bucket
   detergent
   dish-cleaning pad
   matches
   paper napkins
   plastic bags

Use one pot for boiling coffee water, the other for a one-pot stew meal. The frying pan is optional; it is good for fish-frying, pancakes, or bacon and eggs. Use the collapsible bucket to haul water from a nearby stream, or wash pots. Paper napkins are indispensable as plates, cleaners, and fire starters. And plastic bags never run out of uses on kitchen duty.

Thermal bowls are excellent for keeping foods warm on chilly mornings. Detergent can be kept in a 4-ounce poly bottle. Make sure the jackknife is well sharpened before leaving on a trip. And take lots of matches, well protected from weather.

Leave out things like knives, forks, and can openers if everything has been prepackaged.

Dishwashing

This is not a big chore in camp, but clean well to prevent upset stomachs. Do not wash at a stream. Bring up the water in a collapsible bucket. Scour and dry with paper napkins. Occasionally boil cooking and eating utensils clean.

Do not bother to clean blackened pots. Store them in

plastic bags, one stacked in the other. And into the last pot goes matches, pot holder, dish-cleaning pad, paper napkins, and plastic bags.

Garbage Disposal

There is little chance of there being raw garbage on any backpacking trip. Everything is eaten. A day hike will perhaps produce a banana skin or an orange peel, and these should be carried out in a plastic bag. Just about all food packages can be burned, with the exception of aluminum wrappers and cans. Burn aluminum wrappers, pick them from the fire, and pack them out. When using cans (this should and can be avoided), burn the cans, flatten them, and stow in a plastic bag to be carried out. It is a good idea to use a brown paper bag inside that plastic to take the edge off the cans.

Do this garbage cleanup after each meal. Do not carry used and unclean packaging until the next meal. Inevitably a pack will be soiled, and this is an invitation to varmints and bears.

Do not bury garbage, not even burned and flattened cans. Holes are usually shallow. Moreover, it seems that no matter how deep the hole animals will dig up the mess.

Cleanup

Leaving a campsite clean often requires the obliteration of any sign of a campfire. Usually this is a morning chore, when breakfast is done and everyone is anxious to move on. Cleanup is hurried and the job gets half-done. It must not be this way.

Once the fire is doused, rocks thrown aside, and wood strewn about (only leave wood piles at designated campfires), then it is time to drag the area with boots or downed brush. Pick up all the paper and plastic, and pocket it for the next campfire. When leaving a campsite, be sure there is little trace of you left.

chapter nine

Completing The Pack

INCLUDED in every backpacker's gear are items that cannot be easily classified, so they are bunched together under the inclusive heading, Miscellaneous. However, this is not to say that these things are any less important to the backpacker. While some may become optional equipment, other items are necessary and vital in a backpacker's gear. Probably the two most important items are flashlights and line.

Flashlights

Backpackers most often gear their waking hours to daylight. Seldom is there a need to cover the trail in darkness, nor is it advisable. However, in an emergency, or for those night-time camp chores, a reliable flashlight is necessary. Make it a rule never to be without one. And know where it is in your pack!

While there are several sizes of batteries, most are inexpensive and lightweight. Probably the finest for the money are any of the palm-sized flashlights weighing two or three ounces, including their pair of alkaline batteries. They provide remarkable beams through plastic lenses and are very durable. Few metal parts allow for easy maintenance.

Get alkaline batteries. They weigh a little more but give seven times longer service than standard batteries. In cold or hot weather they are extremely efficient, whereas standard batteries are not. Mercury batteries, heavier than alkaline batteries, will last longer and work well in moderate to hot temperatures, but will fail at freezing. Carry an extra set of batteries and an extra bulb. Keep the bulb in with personal items where it is not likely to be crushed.

When packing a flashlight, be sure it is not activated by other gear. A whole day turned on in a pack will make it quite worthless. Frequent and short illuminations are best for any flashlight. This method will allow most chores to be accomplished.

If a flashlight must be used in the dark on a trail, spot flash the trail ahead and go slow.

Headlamps such as those used by spelunkers will free hands for chores, but their excessive weight (1½ lbs.) and cost do not make them a match for a small flashlight at 3 ounces.

Candle lanterns are available for camp use but they, too, are more expensive and heavier than flashlights. They fold flat or telescope to palm size for easy packing, weigh about 8 ounces, and use household candles.

Line

Extra line in the pack is always worth its weight. Use 300-lb. test nylon cord for most backpacking conditions; it will secure flies or tube tents, replace shoelaces, serve as clothesline, hoist food into trees, tie soles to shoes, etc. The list can be endless. In an emergency a nylon cord can tie a splint or even get you across a stream. Fifty feet will weigh about 3 ounces.

Compass

Although a compass is seldom used, it should be included in every pack. Today well-marked trails, excellent guidebooks and maps make it difficult to get into a situation where a compass is needed. However, when hiking into wilderness areas where new and personal trails may be taken, a compass is necessary. Hiking in heavy ground fog may require a direction check. Certainly a compass will come in handy when determining an evening campsite, either to get the morning sun or avoid it.

Several models are available, from the cheap and simple to the expensive encased models. Get one that is waterproof and has a well-defined luminous indicator.

Sunglasses

Any summer hiking can be more enjoyable when wearing sunglasses to lessen eyestrain. They are equally helpful for hiking through snow, rock fields, desert, or alongside a lake. Some of this eyestrain can be obviated if a wide-brim hat is worn. When glasses are used, keep track of them by taking a page from a sailor's notebook: tie a string to the frames and fit it around your head. In heavy forest, where sunglasses tend to darken images, push them up to the forehead.

Sunglasses can also eliminate the surface glare on water and provide an angler with a good look at those trout he is after.

Prescription eyeglasses must be protected. It is best to take along an extra pair with accompanying sunglasses.

Watch

For some the wearing of a watch is unnecessary. They leave watches behind and rely on the sun, learning to estimate time passage and mileage covered even on dark days. When it is light they wake up; they sleep when it is dark, and eat when their stomachs growl. They consider backpacking an occasion to forget the pressure of time.

Others consider a watch a real aid to keeping them organized. Regular rest stops can be made; mileage and time are more accurately measured. Pace can be altered to make up a half-mile, or an extra long lunch rest can be planned with a watch. Cloudy days present no problem to those who have not learned to estimate time passage accurately. For them the frustration of not knowing the time is something they do not need or want.

When wearing a watch backpacking, make sure it is waterproof and shock-resistant. Consider a pocket watch for maximum protection.

More important than the time of day is the day of the week. Once on the trail days have a way of getting lost. Countless events and stimuli make everything run together. Sequences are inevitably mixed up to the point that companions will have to stop and sort out the past three days. Progress and whereabouts become important when expecting a rendezvous for food or joining another party.

Personal Items of Toilet

Toilet items are always a very personal choice. For some it can be an elaborate selection while others seem to get along with a minimum of things. For health reasons unusual preparations are sometimes required. Keep toilet items stored in a transparent plastic bag. Here are basic items to consider:

Soap: a small bar for self and clothing.
Face cloth: try a piece of closed-cell foam.
Toothbrush and paste: break off the brush handle.
Toilet paper: unperfumed, a roll that doubles for kitchen use.

Other items to consider:

Towel: wind and sun, or time, will do the same job.
Deodorant: certainly, if in a group on the trail for more than two days.
Shaving kit: try doing without for a few days.
Comb and brush: mostly for women.
Mirror: for those who shave or use comb; also an emergency signal.

Do not wash directly in streams or lakes, especially in heavy-use areas. No one wants to scoop soapy supper water downstream from a bather. Take the water from the source in a canteen or collapsible bucket. Perhaps a final body rinse could be considered allowable.

Personal Items of Insurance

Carry some identification, at least a driver's license, fire and fishing permits. The customary wallet is fine, but these items wrapped in plastic and stored in a pack bag are less likely to get lost than from a hip pocket. Include cash or travelers checks along with a gasoline credit card. These might get you from a remote road head to civilization without a walk in an emergency.

Take a car key along with that license. Tape and hide another key to the car left at the trail head.

Pipes and cigarettes can be carried in shirt pockets; however, tobacco use should be limited to campfires. Do not smoke on the trail. It is dangerous. Also, cigarette smoking is decidedly offensive to others in the pristine environment of forests and mountains.

Thermometers

Keeping track of air, ground, and water temperatures can be advisable under some conditions: checking advertised capabilities of sleeping bags and clothing, determining the temperatures of snow for wax selection for skis, providing accurate readings of water temperatures that might be too cold to enter (below 50 degrees is dangerous for any prolonged water immersion, even when only wading in streams). Also, determining individual comfort levels can become an interesting study, with dividends in the area of gear paring.

Altimeters

They are expensive items not to be considered for anything but the most professional and technical backpacking. Guidebooks and maps provide enough information to pinpoint any elevation within 100 feet.

Pedometers

These items are worthless. They are totally unreliable in hills and mountains, and little better on the prairies. In fact, they can be very misleading. Do without and rely on maps and guidebooks.

Walking Staff

This is considered an indispensable item to many backpackers. Invariably it becomes a very personal piece of equipment that backpackers are loath to part with. And with good reasons. A 4-foot staff of aluminum or wood can make easier the crossing of streams, working over rock fields or loose gravel, climbing in and out of shallow ditches, moving up or down hills, and assisting others over difficult trails. It can also be used as a trail investigator prodding ahead, a connection to a companion on a fog-bound trail or in the dark, and a campfire destroyer. These staffs are also adequate chin rests, camera tripods, fly center poles, anchors for groundsheets, bush pokers, fire stirrers, and fishing rods.

However, they can be a nuisance. Once a pack is shouldered it is not easy to bend and pick up a staff. Try to remember to prop it against a tree or rock when resting. Or toe-lift it to a waiting hand. Staffs are also a problem when both hands are required to negotiate steep climbs. Unexpected encounters like this may be solved by lowering the staff ahead or raising it after the climb.

When sure of needing both hands, leave the staff at home and field-cut one that can be discarded at any time.

Repair Kits

Once on the trail a hiker is soon many hours and miles away from any place where mending and repairing is just a matter of driving down the street or going to the sewing box. Moreover, equipment breakdowns can be crucial to a backpacker's comfort and welfare. Carry a roll of adhesive nylon fabric for repairing sleeping bags, tents, packbags, and jackets. It is tough, and able to withstand later washing and still remain stuck. Be sure to shape each patch, rounding off the corners where possible.

Needle and threads are indispensable items for repairing socks, pants with split seams, torn pockets, and packs that are separating. Carry heavy nylon thread.

Safety pins are a must, in various sizes.

Rubber cement and patches will be needed if an air mattress is included in a pack.

A set of nesting screwdrivers can be handy.

Rubber bands by the dozen.

Plastic

Various sizes of this ubiquitous material can keep pants and packs dry. It can be used as a private tablecloth, a dry seat on a wet log, a wrapper of soiled clothing, an outer garbage wrap, see-through ditty bag, water carrier, or a waterproof wrapping for fresh-caught trout.

Gear Lists

The selections for basic gear lists are usually quite similar for all backpackers. Individuals will of course have preferences. Conditions to be encountered will dictate equipment to be taken on particular hikes. On an overnight trip in warm weather items like a down jacket can be left behind. Things such as a first aid kit and maps can be left out by some when hiking in a group. Following are the items to be considered basic:

shelter
pack
mattress
raingear
sleeping gear
flashlight w/batteries
maps and guides
nylon line
grate
cooking utensils
canteen
eating utensils
personal items
first aid items
food

Optional items:

> binoculars
> books
> sunglasses
> pedometer
> gloves
> watch
> thermometer
> camera
> stoves
> fishing gear

Personal clothing worn:

> boots
> socks
> pants
> underwear shorts
> ventilating underwear shirts
> wool shirt

Extra clothing in pack:

> socks
> underwear shorts
> T-shirt
> down jacket w/hood

Following is a detailed gear list with weights for any sum-

mer trip where cold weather is a possibility. This same list
will do the job on winter hikes in Florida.

Gear List for Two Hikers on a 3-Day Trip

Item	Weight		Remarks
	lbs.	oz.	
2-man tent	4	0	No. 1 pack
2 day packs	3	4	
2 foam pads	2	12	Tied outside packs
2 rainsuits	1	8	No. 1 pack
sleeping cover	2	0	No. 1 pack (see Chapter 7)
flashlight w/batteries	0	3	No. 1 pack
nylon line, 50 ft.	0	3	No. 1 pack
2 plastic sheets, 36 X 36 in.	0	1	No. 1 pack, day pack rain covers
grate	0	3½	No. 2 pack, tied to bottom
2 quart pots	0	10	No. 2 pack, in plastic bags
quart aluminum bottle, empty	0	6	No. 1 pack
2 thermal bowls	0	2½	No. 2 pack
2 cups	0	1½	No. 2 pack
2 spoons	0	1	No. 2 pack
collapsible bucket	0	4	No. 2 pack
ditty bag	0	4	No. 2 pack
dish-cleaning pad			
pot holder			
matches			

Item	Weight		Remarks
	lbs.	oz.	
paper napkins			
plastic bags			
ditty bag	0	8½	No. 2 pack
scissors			
aspirin			
ace bandage			
first aid kit			(see Chapter 6)
water purification tablets			
snakebite kit			
sun cream			
moleskin			
ditty bag	0	8	No. 2 pack
deodorant			
face-cleaning pads			
soap			
toilet paper			
toothbrushes, paste			
ditty bag	0	6	No. 1 pack
adhesive nylon tape			
extra batteries and bulb			
mirror			
needle and thread			
safety pins			
rubber bands			
compass			
extra clothing in packs			
4 pair socks	0	4	No. 1 pack
2 underwear shorts	0	2	No. 1 pack

Item	Weight		Remarks
	lbs.	oz.	
2 T-shirts	0	4	No. 1 pack
2 down jackets	3	0	No. 1 pack
food for 3 days	6	0	No. 2 pack
Total pack load	27	0	

Clothing Worn on Trail

boots
socks
trousers
underwear
ventilating underwear shirts
wool shirts

Gear Carried in Pockets

compass
sunglasses
maps
watch
utility jackknife (kitchen work)

chapter ten

The Long Trip

SOONER or later most backpackers think of taking a long trip. Reading about and listening to the adventures of those who hike the Muir Trail in the Sierras, or backpack deep into the wilderness areas of the Rocky Mountains, can be very exciting. Those few who complete the entire 2000 miles of the Appalachian Trail in a single summer earn our admiration. Their accomplishments are evidence of singular endurance and imagination, and a constant stimulus to others.

And there is no reason why every backpacker should not consider a long trip once he is sure of his skills. To be sure, there are differences between a long trip and a weekend outing, some of them major, but none that will cause an enthusiastic backpacker to hesitate taking a few weeks in the wilderness.

Where to Go

For our purpose here the long trip will be defined as being
of from two weeks to a month in duration, probably the most
feasible length, considering working men, their vacations,
and employers. Much longer trips can be planned, and they
will reflect similar planning and methods.

Route choices can reflect a backpacker's desire to "get
away from it all," or his wish to cover the spectacular scenery
of high country and deep forests. Sometimes both of these
goals can be accomplished; sections of popular trails become
quite remote once a backpacker gets beyond the range of
weekend hikers.

Perhaps the first long trip to consider would take a backpacker onto well-used trails like the Pacific Crest Trail or
Appalachian Trail. There are advantages here. These trails
are generally well marked, and roads cross them at intervals
or come within a few miles (food caching). Rangers patrol
certain areas and seldom a day passes without meeting someone (safety). These trails generally cover very scenic areas.
The main disadvantage here is that while hiking these well-
used trails there is little chance of being rid of man and his
signs.

A long trip can mean different things regarding routes and
duration. It can be a number of days hiking with occasional
layovers, or it can be a hike into a remote area to be used as
a base camp, with side trips to fish and explore. Or it can be
a combination of these two, taking a backpacker along popular trails but laying over to penetrate more remote areas
by spur trails.

Preparation

Get in touch with the authorities in charge of the area in which you are interested, explain your plan, get an okay and a trail report. If the trail is closed at any point, they will offer alternate routes and perhaps keep you in the same area. Some agencies will furnish a trail résumé, complete with campsite locations.

In some cases this checking can be done the day before, as when planning to use one of the popular trails that are usually in excellent repair. Nevertheless, this may lead to disappointment if the trail is closed. Contacting ahead gives you time to choose another area if the answer is negative to your first query.

Physical Conditioning

Everyone planning a long trip should take the pains to get in shape. Feet and legs will be doing hard service and they must not fail. Practice walking should be vigorous and regular. Those hiking boots must fit. Feel confident that a 20-mile downhill day or a 10-mile uphill day is possible if it becomes necessary.

Safety

More often than not a long trip is an individual or two-man effort. Few people will spend a month away from business and home. And on these long trips trail safety becomes exceedingly important by virtue of the possible remoteness of one's position at the halfway point of a trip.

Even when authorities have been notified, and a disabling accident occurs midway in the hike, the authorities will not be alerted until the day the hikers were supposed to check out of the wilderness. This may be a matter of days. Moreover, it will take a partner those same days to hike out for aid, unless road heads are nearby. On heavily used trails help will ordinarily be close by. However, this too changes with the seasons; spring, fall, and winter find most trails deserted. Trail safety must be practiced at all times. There can be no attitude other than cautious.

Pack

Because of the extended duration, the amount of food, and type of gear, a long trip requires the use of a packframe and bag (see Chapter 3). No other pack will provide the needed volume.

A day pack can be included if short side trips are to be made from a base camp.

Footwear

Be sure that boots are in excellent repair. They must stand up to long miles without failing. Check the stitching carefully. Do not start a hike with boots needing soles.

Camp shoes will be a delightful change of pace here, more so than on any weekend outing.

Socks must be the finest, tried and proven to suit you. Perhaps another pair besides the customary four pair, would be wise in case of loss or wear.

Clothing

When backpacking into wilderness areas, frequently in high country, a hiker must be equipped for all weather conditions. Furious thunderstorms can make a sodden camp for those ill-equipped. And of real concern are sudden summer snows that come with freezing temperatures even in mid-August.

Down clothing and good rain protection are needed even though they may never be used. Items like lightweight wool underwear can make the difference between comfort and misery on a night of unexpected snow.

Shelter

As with the shorter trips there are some who will use tents and others who will rely on flies and tarps. If the latter method is used be sure it will prove adequate for all conditions. There is no changing once three days out and in a storm.

Sleeping bags should be designed to keep you comfortable to an unexpected 15 degrees in western mountains.

Food

Here is one of the major differences between the long and short trips. At 3 pounds of food per day for 2 people, the total food weight for a 3-week trip will be about 63 pounds. This, on top of gear weighing about 33 pounds, is 48 pounds per person. While this will diminish every day out, it may be a little too much to start with. For this reason caching may be necessary.

Miles and days must be calculated and a cache located either on the trail itself, at a road head close to the trail, or where a road crosses the trail. This means getting out ahead in those weeks before the hike.

Package food in air-tight cans wrapped in plastic and buried to discourage rodents and men. As a precaution against accidental discovery, leave a note with the cache: name, destination, and date expected to be by to pick up.

Another way is to rendezvous with someone who will bring supplies. Hiking on a trail like the Appalachian Trail makes this simple in many instances. Also, along some trails there are chances to leave the trail on spurs or highways, and with a short hike find supplies at a town or roadside store.

A stove must certainly be carried for cooking on rainy days, unless plans include meals that can be eaten cooked or uncooked.

Gear Check

Go over that checklist thoroughly. Whereas an item left out on a weekend trip might prove bothersome, it may lead to a lot of misery when missing for two weeks.

Calculate needs carefully. Running short of items can only lead to discomfort. Be sure to have ample supplies of:

> matches
> fuel for stove
> batteries and bulbs
> detergent
> personal soap
> toilet paper

- band-aids
  aspirin
  salt
  sugar

And be sure all gear taken is reliable, proven on the trail, and in top condition.

chapter eleven

Where to Hike

FEW areas of our nation are not accessible by foot. The backpacker can, with courage and good health and time, hike into remote wilderness. There he will confront a primitive environment, learn to live with it and freely take from it more than any grasping technology can obtain for him.

In this wilderness another perspective is apparent. Thinking men readily recognize this. The spirit senses primal relationships so easily forgotten in a modern society. In the light of nature's splendor and power men quickly accept that they are just men, a part of life that is as meaningful as all other parts, certainly uniquely aware and therefore charged with the responsibility to see that all men in time to come will enjoy these benefits. Men must preserve this retreat; all men should experience it.

Generally, backpacking trips take place on federal and state-owned lands, in various parks, forest and wilderness areas. At the start of 1967 there were about 88,000 miles of trails on federal lands with plans to increase this to 125,000. Another 15,000 miles were state-administered, with 12,000 more planned. In 1967 the Outdoor Recreation Resources Review Commission estimated that by the year 2000 there will be 125 million occasions of hiking participation each year. A great number of these will be backpacking excursions.

Most of the trails are well defined and in good repair. Many of them have restrictions to preserve the land, yet allow the entire population to enjoy their own kind of recreation.

TRAIL MILEAGE ON FEDERAL AND STATE LANDS

State	Total	Foot	Horseback	Bicycle	Trail Scooter
Alaska	1,142	1,142	702	41	88
Arizona	5,269	4,690	5,078	5	1,331
Arkansas	1,447	1,367	550	0	407
California	17,423	17,046	15,593	454	5,247
Colorado	11,114	11,024	11,054	305	1,820
Connecticut	507	500	7	0	0
Florida	188	169	98	12	35
Hawaii	455	176	332	0	0
Idaho	10,817	10,817	8,859	1,006	4,498
Illinois	423	252	227	0	0
Indiana	298	147	151	1	0
Iowa	109	66	43	0	0
Kentucky	257	218	0	0	0
Maine	576	517	60	0	0
Maryland	368	331	201	184	0

State	Total	Foot	Horseback	Bicycle	Trail Scooter
Massachusetts	214	85	129	0	0
Michigan	869	490	268	193	0
Minnesota	336	327	38	22	15
Missouri	246	176	119	0	0
Montana	9,328	9,328	7,352	630	844
Nevada	2,088	1,656	1,523	110	953
New Hampshire	1,008	1,008	200	25	50
New Jersey	379	329	58	8	0
New Mexico	4,124	3,987	4,024	4	1,000
New York	1,001	906	54	47	0
North Carolina	1,431	1,416	538	0	0
Ohio	438	238	200	1	0
Oklahoma	148	79	59	10	0
Oregon	5,546	5,205	4,765	506	2,188
Pennsylvania	4,426	4,372	56	0	0
Tennessee	723	702	168	0	0
Texas	379	153	209	17	0
Utah	4,451	3,796	4,197	357	2,944
Vermont	302	302	89	0	0
Virginia	1,284	1,217	367	100	200
Washington	7,488	7,488	6,555	530	2,916
West Virginia	786	736	280	125	175
Wisconsin	278	242	36	0	0
Wyoming	5,146	5,146	5,098	149	644

Included in this trail mileage are several trail systems, small and large, all of them unique in terrain and history. A few bear the names of people who sacrificed and worked to see them become a reality.

The Big Ones

The following trails are ones presently considered the longest by virtue of design and miles completed to date. Many other trails have been proposed and are being designed.

Appalachian Trail

This trail is the best known of all trails. It extends more than 2000 miles along America's eastern backbone. From Mt. Katahdin in Maine to Springer Mountain in Georgia it passes through 13 states. Some of it is in densely populated areas. It is easily accessible and can be used for a casual day hike or a three-month adventure. It is well marked and described foot by foot in guidebooks prepared by Appalachian Trail Conference members. Shelters are provided along nearly its entire length at approximately 8-mile intervals, or a day's hike. In some areas these shelters and commercial accommodations allow for trips to be planned without packing a tent or food.

Every manner of terrain will be encountered: level forest trails and rugged mountain climbs that will test the most accomplished backpacker.

In Maine the trail passes through a wilderness of lakes, streams, and mountains. In New Hampshire hikers cross the White Mountains, crest the Presidential Range, and meander into Vermont through rural areas; then they go on to the Green Mountains and the Long Trail. The trail is very popular in Vermont and New Hampshire, well used and noted for its excellent accommodations.

In Massachusetts the trail climbs Mount Greylock and

moves into the Berkshire Hills through scenic valleys and woods to northwestern Connecticut, where the route is through state forests. In New York the trail is rather short, crossing the Schaghticoke Mountain area into the Harlem Valley and across the Hudson River at Bear Mountain Bridge to the Palisades Interstate Park. This is the oldest section of the trail.

In New Jersey the trail follows a crest along the Kittatinny mountains to Delaware Water Gap and Pennsylvania. Passing sites of forts used during the French and Indian Wars, north of Harrisburg the trail crosses the Susquehanna River into rural valleys and the southern Pennsylvania highlands.

In Maryland the trail follows a ridge crest, crosses the Chesapeake and Ohio Canal Towpath, and reaches historic Harpers Ferry. Once in Virginia, passing through areas of Civil War interest, the trail follows the Blue Ridge through Shenandoah National Park. It is easily reached by the Skyline Drive, which parallels the trail. North of Roanoke the trail moves westward and south into the higher mountains of Tennessee and North Carolina. From here on are the most rugged and wild parts of the trail. The trail passes through the Great Smoky Mountains National Park and dips sharply to the Little Tennessee River and Fontana Dam. It bends east and south to Georgia and back again to its terminus at Springer Mountain, Georgia.

For information and guidebooks contact:

Appalachian Trail Conference
1718 N Street, N.W.
Washington, D.C. 20036

Pacific Crest Trail

This trail is over 2300 miles long, truly a high-country trail cresting ridges and mountains most of its length. It is well marked and easily traveled by foot or pack animal. However, accommodations similar to those of the Appalachian Trail are scarce. Few highways cross the trail as it extends southward through spectacular scenery, our land's tallest and oldest trees, highest mountains, and most abundant wildlife.

In Washington the trail follows the high ridges of the Cascade Mountains, the most rugged and primitive area in America. This is a land of high, barren ridges, splendid vistas of mountain ranges, snow-covered peaks and glaciers, alpine meadows and lakes. Dense stands of Douglas fir reach up the western slopes.

At the Columbia River the trail crosses the Bridge of Gods into Oregon and climbs the Cascade crest again. The going is easier here through fir forests, along streams and lake shores. It passes Mt. Hood, Mt. Jefferson, the Three Sisters, and Crater Lake.

In California the trail reaches the high ridges of the Sierra Nevada with its magnificent scenery and Mt. Whitney. Here the trail is high and difficult in parts. Lassen Volcanic, Yosemite, Sequoia, and Kings Canyon national parks are passed on the way to the Mojave Desert and the Sierra Madre and San Bernadino ranges. The trail ends at the Mexico border.

For information contact:

Pacific Crest Trail System Conference
Hotel Green
Pasadena, California

Florida Trail

This 600-mile trail extends from Everglades City in southern Florida to Panama City in the state's western panhandle. Hiking the trail is an invigorating experience. It is the only one of our nation's trails to offer the uniqueness of primitive cypress swamps dressed with wild orchids, grassy savannas swept by cool winds, broad prairies of palmetto, and rolling hills covered with pine forests. A bandshell blue sky stretches to all horizons. While the rest of the nation shivers in snow, hikers on the Florida Trail are removing their sweaters to soak up sunshine.

The trail begins in south Florida on the Tamiami Trail about four miles east of Monroe Station at the Oasis Airport, heads north into the wilderness of Big Cypress Swamp, and crosses the Everglades Parkway (Alligator Alley) at Mile 39. It continues north through the swamps and savannas of The Devils Gardens to cross the Caloosahatchee River at Ortona. Near Palmdale the trail turns east along Fisheating Creek and on to Lake Okeechobee, where the trail mounts dikes and presses around the north shore of the lake. It extends north from the lake to follow the west side of the upper reaches of the St. Johns River. By this time pine and palmetto have replaced cypress and savannas. The trail stays east of Orlando and crosses Interstate 4 south of Sanford. Here it crosses the Wekiva River and moves into the forests of Ocala National Forest. Leaving Ocala National Forest, the trail heads north to Gold Head State Park and then Osceola National Forest. Here the trail bends west, joins the Suwannee River and takes a short turn south along the riverbanks until it breaks west again to Wakulla Springs and the rolling hills south of Tallahassee. It reaches Apalachicola National Forest and finally its present terminal at Panama City on the Gulf of Mexico.

For maps, guides, and information on completed sections of the trail contact:

> Florida Trail Association, Inc.
> 33 S.W. 18th Terrace
> Miami, Florida 33129

Other long trails exist for the backpacker. The Long Trail is a well-known route, a north-south trail running through Vermont for 255 miles. Contact the Green Mountain Club, 63 Center Street, Rutland, Vermont. The Horseshoe Trail in Pennsylvania is a 120-mile path from Valley Forge to the Appalachian Trail on Sharp Mountain. Contact the Horseshoe Trail Club, 1600 Three Penn Center Plaza, Philadelphia, Pennsylvania 19102. The Baker Trail is 100 miles long in Pennsylvania, starting at Freeport and moving north to Cook Forest State Park. Contact Pittsburgh Council of American Youth Hostels, 6300 Fifth Avenue, Pittsburgh, Pennsylvania 15232.

Shorter trails are found in our National Parks System. Because of excellent base camp accommodations, these trails provide good day trips for beginners. Long outings are also possible. Although somewhat crowded, some of these trails offer unsurpassed scenery and relatively easy going. For trail information contact the following parks:

Big Bend National Park
Big Bend, Texas 79834

Crater Lake National Park
Box 672
Medford, Oregon 97501

Glacier National Park
West Glacier, Montana 59936

Grand Canyon National Park
Box 129
Grand Canyon, Arizona 86032

Grand Teton National Park
Box 67
Moose, Wyoming 83012

Great Smoky Mountains National Park
Gatlinburg, Tennessee 37738

Kings Canyon National Park
Three Rivers, California 93271

Lassen Volcanic National Park
Mineral, California 96063

Mount Rainier National Park
Longmore, Washington 98397

Olympic National Park
600 East Park Avenue
Port Angeles, Washington 98362

Rocky Mountain National Park
Estes Park, Colorado 80517

Sequoia National Park
Three Rivers, California 93271

Shenandoah National Park
Luray, Virginia 22835

Yosemite National Park
Box 577
Yosemite, California 95389

Zion National Park
Springdale, Utah 84767

In addition to the National Parks System other federal lands such as national forests have developed trails to be used by foot, pack animals, and motor vehicles. By writing the following regional headquarters, information can be obtained about a forest and its trails. These forests include Primitive (P) and Wilderness (W) Areas.

PACIFIC NORTHWEST REGION
P.O. Box 3623
Portland, Oregon 96208

Diamond Peak, Oregon (W)
Eagle Cap, Oregon (W)
Gearhart Mountain, Oregon (W)
Glacier Peak, Washington (W)
Goat Rocks, Washington (W)
Kalmiopsis, Oregon (W)
Mount Adams, Washington (W)
Mount Hood, Oregon (W)
Mount Jefferson, Oregon (P)
Mountain Lakes, Oregon (W)
North Cascades, Washington (P)
Strawberry Mountain, Oregon (W)
Three Sisters, Oregon (W)

CALIFORNIA REGION
630 Sansome Street
San Francisco, California 94111

Agua Tibia, California (P)
Caribou, California (W)
Desolation Valley, California (P)
Devil Canyon-Bear Canyon, California (P)
Dome Lant, California (W)
Emigrant Basin, California (P)
High Sierra, California (P)
Hoover, California and Nevada (W)
John Muir, California (W)
Marble Mountain, California (W)
Minarets, California (W)
Mokelumne, California (W)
San Gorgonio, California (W)
San Jacinto, California (W)
San Rafael, California (P)
South Warner, California (W)
Thousand Lakes, California (W)
Ventana, California (P)
Yolla Bolly-Middle Eel, California (W)

INTERMOUNTAIN REGION
Forest Service Building
Ogden, Utah 84403

Bridger, Wyoming (W)
High Uintas, Utah (P)
Hoover, Colorado and Nevada (W)

Idaho, Idaho (P)
Jarbidge, Nevada (W)
Sawtooth, Idaho (P)
Teton, Wyoming (W)

NORTHERN REGION
Federal Building
Missoula, Montana 59801

Absaroka, Montana (P)
Anaconda-Pintlar, Montana (W)
Beartooth, Montana (P)
Bob Marshall, Montana (W)
Cabinet Mountains, Montana (W)
Gates of the Mountains, Montana (W)
Mission Mountains, Montana (P)
Salmon River Breaks, Idaho (P)
Selway-Bitterroot, Idaho and Montana (W)
Spanish Peaks, Montana (P)

ROCKY MOUNTAIN REGION
Federal Center, Building 85
Denver, Colorado 80225

Cloud Peak, Wyoming (P)
Flat Tops, Colorado (P)
Glacier, Wyoming (P)
Gore Range-Eagle Nest, Colorado (P)
La Garita, Colorado (W)
Maroon Bells-Snowmass, Colorado (W)

North Absaroka, Wyoming (W)
Popo Agie, Wyoming (P)
Rawah, Colorado (W)
San Juan, Colorado (P)
South Absaroka, Wyoming (W)
Stratified, Wyoming (P)
Uncompahgre, Colorado (P)
Upper Rio Grande, Colorado (P)
West Elk, Colorado (W)
Wilson Mountains, Colorado (P)
Mt. Zirkel, Colorado (W)

SOUTHWESTERN REGION
Federal Building
Albuquerque, New Mexico 87101

Black Range, New Mexico (P)
Blue Range, Arizona (P)
Chiricahua, Arizona (W)
Galiuro, Arizona (W)
Gila, New Mexico (W)
Mazatzal, Arizona (W)
Mount Baldy, Arizona (P)
Pecos, New Mexico (W)
Pine Mountain, Arizona (P)
San Pedro Parks, New Mexico (W)
Sierra Ancha, Arizona (W)
Superstition, Arizona (W)
Sycamore Canyon, Arizona (P)
Wheeler Mountain, New Mexico (W)
White Mountain, New Mexico (W)

NORTH CENTRAL REGION
710 North 6th Street
Milwaukee, Wisconsin 53203

Boundary Water Canoe Area, Minnesota (P)

EASTERN REGION
6816 Market Street
Upper Darby, Pennsylvania 19082

Great Gulf, New Hampshire (W)

SOUTHERN REGION
50 Seventh Street N.E.
Atlanta, Georgia 30323

Linville Gorge, North Carolina (W)

Other Ways To Travel

Using essentially backpacking gear lists and techniques, a
person can now enjoy a variety of outdoor holidays on water
and land.

The Pack Trip

Horses do the heavy work here, leaving more energy for
angling and the like, but less money in the wallet. Pack trips
can be taken anywhere in the land where horse trails are provided. Horses can be rented and, using lightweight gear, a
person can eliminate the pack horse. Compartmentalized

bags designed to fit behind a western saddle are available from one manufacturer.

This go-it-alone outing is nothing like the restrictive trips organized by commercial outfitters.

The Canoe Trip

Canoeing for a day will take anyone into complete wilderness in the beautiful lake country of the Boundary Waters Canoe Area in northern Minnesota, or the lakes of Maine and Yellowstone National Park. A rented canoe, maps, and lightweight gear are all that is needed to enjoy a quiet weekend on any of the many wild rivers in our land. Whitewater trips will take a person beyond the noise of motorboats. See the following:

CANOEING-CAMPING IN THE BOUNDARY WATERS
  CANOE AREA
USFS Federal Building
Duluth, Minnesota 55801

ADIRONDACK CANOE ROUTES
William G. Howard, M.F.
State of New York Conservation Department
Albany, New York

WILDERNESS BOATING ON YELLOWSTONE LAKES
Superintendent
Yellowstone National Park
Wyoming, 83020

Other mechanical means are employed to get people into

the wilderness. Leisurely float-trips down rivers, boat-cruising on lakes, jeep travel into rugged desert country, air travel to the Far North, airboat and swamp buggy rides into the Florida wilderness.

All of these usually require an expense not found in the previously described modes of transportation. However, they do provide a swift way of getting to remote areas and some may feel this is worth the cost.

chapter twelve

Reference Information

EQUIPMENT suppliers are many and widely located throughout the country. All will supply a catalog on request and fill mail orders or advise of companies handling their brand of equipment.

One word of advice: be patient when ordering. Almost without exception they will at one time or another foul up an order, send it piecemeal, not have the items in stock, or take longer than expected even when extra money was sent for airmail special handling.

Investigate and compare before buying. It will be worth the effort in money saved and well spent.

Equipment Suppliers

Following is a partial list of suppliers, all of them carrying excellent equipment.

ALPINE HUT
4725 30th Avenue N.E.
Seattle, Washington 98122
(complete line of various manufacturers)

ALP SPORT, INC.
3235-45 Prairie Avenue (P.O. Box 1081)
Boulder, Colorado 80302
(clothing, packs, sleeping bags, tents at dealers throughout
the country)

BILL JACKSON, INC.
1120 4th Street South
St. Petersburg, Florida 33701
(complete line of various manufacturers)

CAMP TRAILS
3920 West Clarendon
Phoenix, Arizona 85019
(clothing, packs, tents at dealers throughout the country)

COLORADO OUTDOOR SPORT CORPORATION
P.O. Box 5544
Denver, Colorado 80217
(complete line of Gerry equipment at dealers throughout
the country)

EASTERN MOUNTAIN SPORTS, INC.
1041 Commonwealth Avenue
Boston, Massachusetts 02215
(complete line of various manufacturers)

HOLUBAR
P.O. Box 7
Boulder, Colorado 80302
(complete line)

KELTY PACK
1801 Victory Boulevard
Glendale, California 91201
(complete line of various manufacturers)

LEISURE PRODUCTS COMPANY
1516 West 55th Street
La Grange, Illinois 60525
(paper sleeping bags and linen)

MOOR AND MOUNTAIN
14 Main Street
Concord, Massachusetts 01742
(complete line of various manufacturers)

MORSAN
810 Route 17
Paramus, New Jersey 07652
(complete line of various manufacturers)

OCATE CORPORATION
P.O. Box 2368
Santa Fe, New Mexico 87501
(tents and polyfoam mittens, mukluks, sleeping bags)

RECREATIONAL EQUIPMENT, INC. (a cooperative)
1525 11th Avenue
Seattle, Washington 98122
(complete line of various manufacturers)

SIERRA DESIGNS
4th and Addison Streets
Berkeley, California 94710
(complete line)

SKI HUT
16115 University Avenue
Berkeley, California 94703
(complete line of Trailwise equipment)

Food Suppliers

Many of the above-listed equipment suppliers can also furnish food items. However, there are suppliers who specialize in this area, and while their prices are comparable, the food specialists listed below do provide a greater selection. They are considerably more prompt in filling orders than are the equipment suppliers.

Following is a partial list of suppliers:

CHUCK WAGON FOODS
176 Oak Street
Newton, Massachusetts

DRI-LITE FOODS
11333 Atlantic
Lynwood, California 90263

RICHMOOR CORPORATION
616 North Robertson Boulevard
Los Angeles, California 90069

STOW-A-WAY PRODUCTS
103 Ripley Road
Cohasset, Massachusetts 12125

Hiking Organizations

Of interest to a backpacker in America are about 150 organizations and clubs with their chapters and affiliations. For some 200,000 walkers, hikers, and backpackers these organizations provide the machinery for group outings, technical information, maps, and guides. Conservation is fundamental with them. Anyone beginning to backpack will certainly appreciate their available guidance and information.

Following is a partial list of organizations. Contact them for addresses of local clubs and affiliations.

THE APPALACHIAN TRAIL CONFERENCE
1718 N Street, N.W.
Washington, D.C. 20036

THE FEDERATION OF WESTERN OUTDOOR CLUBS
Route 3 (P.O. Box 172)
Carmel, California 93921

THE FLORIDA TRAIL ASSOCIATION
33 S.W. 18th Terrace
Miami, Florida 33129

SIERRA CLUB
1050 Mills Tower, 270 Bush Street
San Francisco, California 94104

Other Books for Backpackers

The Complete Walker by Colin Fletcher
Backpack Techniques by Ruth Dyar Mendenhall
Home in Your Pack by Bradford Angier

Maps and Guides

Many guidebooks are available at libraries and bookstores. Some suppliers list numerous trail guidebooks.

An excellent general guidebook is *The Handbook of Wilderness Travel* by George S. Wells.

Area maps are often included in guidebooks, but for detailed information it is best to obtain topographical maps available at most equipment suppliers, Forest Service offices, or national park visitor centers. Or write to:

U.S. Geodetic Survey
Denver, Colorado 80225

U.S. Geodetic Survey
Washington, D.C. 20242

Index

(Note: Numbers in Italics refer to illustrations.)